Daffodil

Daffodil

The remarkable story of the world's most popular spring flower

Noel Kingsbury with photographs by Jo Whitworth

Timber Press   London   Portland

Frontispiece: 'Bunting' AGM. Photo by Jo Whitworth.

Published in 2013 by Timber Press, Inc.

The Haseltine Building   6a Lonsdale Road
133 S.W. Second Avenue, Suite 450   London NW6 6RD
Portland, Oregon 97204-3527   timberpress.co.uk
timberpress.com

Printed in China
Book design by Patrick Barber

Library of Congress Cataloging-in-Publication Data

Kingsbury, Noel.
    Daffodil: the remarkable story of the world's most popular spring
flower/Noel Kingsbury; with photographs by Jo Whitworth.—1st ed.
        p.   cm.
    Includes bibliographical references and index.
    ISBN 978-1-60469-318-8
    1. Daffodils. 2. Daffodils—History. I. Whitworth, Jo. II. Title.
    SB413.D12+
    584'.34—dc23   2012037996

A catalog record for this book is also available from the British Library.

Contents

Acknowledgements

THIS BOOK was photographer Jo Whitworth's idea (she has a family connection with the Backhouses), but it grew naturally out of my interest in the history of plant breeding, and indeed in daffodils. So first of all I must thank Jo and Rob Whitworth for the idea and their commitment to this project.

I'm very grateful to Kate and Duncan Donald for their hospitality when I visited them at Croft 16 in the Scottish Highlands (and in driving me eighty miles to and from the nearest airport) and their help in answering my questions; to Joy Uings, for passing her dissertation on Edward Leeds on to me; to Charles Chesshire, for various insights into the Williams family of Cornwall; to Robert W. Scotland, for sending me a preliminary of his paper on the origin of the daffodil corona; to RHS Daffodil Registrar Sharon McDonald, for answering various questions; to Chris Braithwaite at Acorn Bank, Cumbria; to David Beuch at Cotehele; to John Lanyon, whose previous work at Cotehele was how Jo and I got started on this daffodil enterprise; and to Chris Bligh, who has done so much to promote the conservation of the feral daffodils of Gloucestershire's Golden Triangle. Normally, when researching and writing a book like this, the RHS Lindley Library in London would be the first port of call; unfortunately a minor fire (but with much smoke) in August 2011 resulted in its closure for many months. I managed a short visit to the building site, thanks to Barbara Collecott, Liz Gilbert, and other staff. Daffseek.org has been an invaluable source of advice, so thank you to Nancy Tackett and Ben Blake, the website administrators.

I am grateful to the breeders featured in the book who answered my questions and supplied pictures illustrating their work: Ron Scamp, Elise and Richard Havens, Brent and Becky Heath, Bob Spotts, and Harold Koopowitz.

It has been good to work with Timber Press again, and Anna Mumford as commissioning editor should be congratulated on seeing the potential in the concept of this book; thanks also to all the other Timber staff who worked on it. Finally, my wife, Jo Eliot, has been her usual loving and supportive self during my work on the project.

JO WHITWORTH would like to thank the following people and locations for their generous help with the photography for this book: Kate and Duncan Donald at Croft 16 Daffodils, Wester Ross, Scotland; Brodie Castle, Forres, Scotland (National Trust for Scotland); Ron Scamp at Quality Daffodils, Cornwall; Jo Selman, Tamar Valley, Cornwall; New Generation Daffodils, Cornwall; Fentongollan Farm, Cornwall; Broadleigh Gardens, Somerset; Great Dixter, East Sussex; Sutton Court, Hereford; Farndale Nature Reserve, North Yorkshire; Sharon McDonald, RHS International Daffodil Registrar; Chris Bligh, Kempley, Gloucestershire; The Daffodil Society; Woodborough Nursery and Daffodil Pick-Your-Own, Pewsey, Wiltshire; RHS Gardens at Wisley and Rosemoor, and The National Trust. And a special thank you to Rob Whitworth for all his help and advice.

PRELIMINARY NOTES

Three acronyms are used:

RHS = Royal Horticultural Society (of the United Kingdom)

AGM = Award of Garden Merit (given by the RHS)

USDA = United States Department of Agriculture

Often when a daffodil variety is mentioned, its division is given (these are explained in the first chapter), its breeder named (if known), and the date provided for its first flowering (for older varieties) or when it was first registered with the RHS. This information is offered either in accompanying text or, if not, in parentheses after the name.

All months apply to the temperate Northern Hemisphere. Those in the Southern Hemisphere will need to convert months to their "opposites."

Daffseek.org is the authority for names.

Calculations for converting historical prices to modern ones were made using this site: measuringworth.com/ukcompare.

Daffodils and their place in our culture

Daffodils are somehow the quintessential spring flower. The appearance of their distinctive yellow blooms is a sure sign that winter has either ended or is about to soon. Unlike the tulip, which appears to be dependent on us for its continued re-emergence in the garden, daffodils reappear faithfully every year; and not just in the garden but in places such as roadsides, churchyards, and parks where they have been planted, often decades ago—in some cases over a century ago. These plants are clearly great survivors, thriving even in places where they have obviously been accidentally dropped or discarded—the flowers frequently mark where someone emptied the back of their car of garden waste into a ditch or hedge, little thinking that the event and scene of their crime would be annually and flamboyantly marked for

There are around twenty-seven thousand unique cultivars of daffodil. Unlike other flowers—roses, tulips, orchids, whose numbers of deliberately bred varieties range across great swathes of the spectrum or show off an extravagant range of shapes—daffodils are remarkably alike. All single cultivars have the same basic shape—a cup (also called a corona) and petals (although botanists do not call them petals); even the doubles or the strange "split-corona" varieties easily betray their basic inheritance. Above all there is the colour, more or less every shade of yellow which can be imagined, but very little else: white of course, but then almost every flower has at least one white variant, some flashes of orange, but never very much, and that's it; there are so-called pink varieties, but they are more of a tan-apricot. One of the fascinating things about daffodils is just how much play we can have with the same basic design and the same colour scheme, about how much breeders, the bulb trade, and we—the customers—keep on coming back for more, as if we can never leave this most successful design alone.

At the heart of this book is the idea of the daffodil as a metaphor for our relationship with nature, as being a cultivated plant, but one which is capable of also living its own life. Like cats, they feel only partly domesticated. The book is as much about the daffodil as

cultural icon as it is about the daffodil as garden plant. Daffodils appear in paintings and in poetry, as emblems of spring and of nature. This cultural status is surely a large part of their appeal; we buy them as tight buds from florists as early as we can at the end of the winter not just because we know they will be pretty and yellow, but because Wordsworth and other poets wrote about them, and they appear endlessly reproduced as a sign of spring at every level of art from the museum-hung masterpiece to souvenir-shop kitsch. The daffodil cut-flower industry is a big one, and historically it was something of a pioneer in the craft and business of how to transfer the golden promise of spring several hundred miles, from the field to the vase on the table. The social history of this industry is part of this book too, as it has been an important driver in directing how daffodils have been bred and appreciated.

At the core of our relationship with the daffodil is how we have changed and moulded it. The key person here is the breeder. Breeders have historically been

Large colonies of daffodils are a common feature of gardens and parks throughout the temperate zone. Here at Great Dixter, in Sussex, the nineteenth-century variety 'Princeps' flourishes in a garden which may have been one of the first to grow daffodils on this scale, "naturalised" in grass ▪1, ▪2. In other gardens, such as Acorn Bank, Cumbria, daffodils have spread through the woods more through natural processes than active planting ▪3. ▶

rather shy and retiring people, leaving little of historical record. Daffodil breeders have been rather the exception, in that their names tend to be better known. They are a colourful lot, and it is the intention here to make them central to the daffodil story.

Why are daffodils special? I believe that there are three factors which make them so.

1) **A BIOLOGICAL FACTOR.** Daffodils are true perennials. Some of the plants sold as perennials (as herbaceous or bulbous) have, in truth, a limited lifespan. Among bulbs, tulips and lilies are a case in point. In ideal conditions, they may live for quite a few years, but they do not go on forever and, crucially, have a limited ability to form clumps. Daffodils are not only immensely long-lived but continually clone themselves to form ever-expanding clumps. They are the bulb

equivalent of those robust border perennials like hardy geraniums or goldenrod, whose clumps just keep on getting bigger and bigger.

2) **A HISTORICAL FACTOR.** Daffodils are an imperial flower. Flourishing in the climate of Great Britain, the plants rode the coattails of the British Empire, but really only to those lands where people of British descent chose to settle, inevitably ones with a climate similar to back home. The reasons for this are endlessly debated by historians, but what became an anglophone or Anglo-American culture ended up dominating the world. The daffodil is part of that culture.

3) **A SOCIAL AND CULTURAL FACTOR.** The daffodil is a cult flower. All gardening cultures choose particular plants and try to "improve" them. It is, however, really only the British (and their cultural descendants) and the Japanese who have produced cult plants. Cult flowers attract enthusiasts, who collect, categorise, and name their chosen plant and, crucially, continually select and breed new ones. Shows and competitions are central to the cult plant. Cult plants appeal to people with an obsessive streak.

Historically, auriculas, polyanthus, ranunculus, tulips, and dianthus were important cult plants in northern Europe. It was originally the Dutch who grew them (and, in the case of tulips, became famously obsessed), but the Dutch commercial interest took over, and the amateur enthusiasm was left to the British. By the late nineteenth century, these "florist's flowers," as they were known, were being replaced by other cult plants: dahlias, sweet peas, chrysanthemums—and daffodils.

Many cult plant enthusiasts will grow only the objects of their obsession and never let a cabbage or a rose enter their gardens. Cult plants attract a wide range of people, but (until recently) nearly all were men, with a strong tendency for growers to be part of what could broadly be called the skilled working class. Some of the cult plant growers are true obsessives, and given to a clannish secretiveness; I am told this is particularly true of Japanese growers. In researching this book I found the daffodil fraternity immensely friendly and helpful, but there was the odd hint that secrets were held, and one well-known breeder point-blank refused to talk to me, saying "I've never heard of you in connection with daffodils."

'Ormeau' **1** is one of many thousands of daffodil varieties which fit the popular idea of what a daffodil is; it was bred by W. J. Dunlop in Northern Ireland sometime before 1949. 'Winifred van Graven' (Van Graven Bros., Netherlands, pre-1954) **2**, 'Gem of Antrim' (Tom Bloomer, Northern Ireland, 1964) **3**, and 'Spencer Tracy' (J. W. A. Lefeber, Netherlands, pre-1943) **4** all look pretty similar to most of the gardening public, whereas daffodil connoisseurs will instantly spot many differences. Much real distinctiveness in daffodils comes through mutations, such as doubling, as in 'Yellow Cheerfulness' **5**, first grown (pre-1937) by the Dutch company Eggink Bros. Split-coronas, such as 'Menehay' (Ron Scamp, UK, 1991) **6**, are also a mutation, popular as a cut flower but not appreciated by many gardeners, who see them as deformed.

Glimmers from the past

NAMING A FLOWER

WHEN WE LOOK at the words used for daffodils we have to think ourselves out of our familiar world. We are very focussed on flowers—we grow flowers, we buy cut flowers, and flower imagery surrounds us. Our ancestors would not have enjoyed flowers in this way; for them, often hungry or suffering from ailments now easily cured, such uses would have seemed irrelevant, compared to what were far more important uses for plants: food, flavorings for food, and medicine.

The name "daffodil" and its variants (daffodily, daffadowndilly, afody, affodily) are thought to have been derived from the Latin *asphodilus*, a group of plants of largely Mediterranean origin, unrelated to daffodils and whose flowers bear no resemblance whatsoever to them, being similar only in having bulbs and strap-like leaves. Also classed as a daffodil was the snakehead fritillary (*Fritillaria meleagris*); English herbalist John Gerard, whose *Herball* of 1597 is a major source of early plant knowledge and lore, referred to it as the "Checquered Daffodill." We would see no resemblance now, and even their bulbs look totally dissimilar. Oddly, at least to us, the "wild daffodil" of Britain, the one we now know as *Narcissus pseudonarcissus*, was dubbed the "bastard" daffodil, i.e., a false daffodil, not the real thing. That it did not even

have its own name must indicate that it was a comparatively rare plant, and one which had little use.

"Daffodil" in most English usages is used to refer to the classic florist and garden daffodil pattern: single flowers with a big trumpet-like cup, usually yellow. Anything else tends to get called "narcissus." There is no rationale behind this, and it makes life simpler if all members of the botanical genus *Narcissus* get called the same—daffodil. "Narcissus" is derived from the Greek *narco* ("becoming numb"), the same root as the word "narcotic." Here then is a hint of one of the few uses to which daffodils were put in traditional herbal medicine. Gerard refers to the classical Greek writer Sophocles calling them "the garland of the great infernall goddes, bicause they that are diparted and dulled with death, should woorthily be crowned with a dulling flower." The Furies, vengeful spirits of the underworld in Greek mythology, wore daffodils in their tangled hair and used them to stupefy their victims.

The word "narcissus" is linked inexorably with that of the beautiful boy Narcissus in Greek mythology, who was unaware of the intense love for him felt by the wood nymph Echo, who was cursed by being only able to repeat his last words. Eventually she pined away for him to such an extent that she became only a faint voice in the woods. As a revenge and punishment on Narcissus, Venus, the god of love, sent Cupid to cast a spell over him, so that he would fall in love with the first face he saw. What happened, of course, is that he leaned over a pool to drink and fell in love with his own image. Like Echo, he began to waste away with unrequited love, but the gods took pity on him, and turned him into a flower—a daffodil, probably *Narcissus tazetta*, which we know to have been grown in ancient Greece. Not surprisingly, daffodils came to symbolize both unrequited love and egotism in the Victorian language of flowers, and narcissism has come to mean a pathological sense of preening self-worth.

A more sinister legend, one probably linked to a folk understanding of rape, abduction, and bride-kidnapping, is that of Persephone and Pluto. Persephone was a beautiful young woman who stopped one day to pick a daffodil and was kidnapped by Pluto, god of the underworld. However, a deal was struck and she was allowed back to the surface every year—her mother Ceres (goddess of agriculture) making the daffodil and other plants flower in spring at the time her incarceration would end.

Daffodils have been a symbol of spring and rebirth in many cultures, not just because that is when they flower, but because of their persistence in coming back every year. In **1**, daffodils grown in fields for cut flowers in the Tamar Valley in Cornwall have survived long after cultivation was abandoned. In parts of Britain daffodils appear to be wild but have almost certainly spread from cultivation centuries ago **2**, blending in with native wildflowers, such as wood anemone (*Anemone nemorosa*) **3**. Cultivated daffodils are descended from several different species; in the Tamar Valley, varieties clearly descended from the white Mediterranean *Narcissus poeticus* have established themselves in hedge banks after being discarded from cultivation **4**, **5**. ▶

Beauty and the beast

GOOD AND ILL WITH DAFFODIL CHEMISTRY

THE ASSOCIATION of the daffodil with a narcotic state indicates one possible use for daffodils in distant times gone by. A narcotic state and convulsions are among the symptoms of daffodil poisoning, along with nausea and severe abdominal pain, so it is not surprising, perhaps, that there is comparatively little record of the use of daffodils in traditional herbal medicine. The Romans are known to have used the plant as a poultice for wounds, although the sap contains an irritant, calcium oxalate, so one doubts if it did much good! Galen, the second-century Greek medical writer, is quoted by Gerard as saying that "the roots of Narcissus have such wonderful qualities of drying [presumably he means its astringency] that they consound and glew together very great wounds, yea and such gashes or cuts as happen about the veins, sinues, and tendons." Maud Grieve's encyclopedic *A Modern Herbal* (1931) gives the plant little space, mentioning only occasional use for treating dysentery and bronchial catarrh.

There are some intriguing links between ancient monastic sites in Britain and large populations of *Narcissus pseudonarcissus* or *N. obvallaris*. For example, it is said that the only large population of wild daffodils in the London area is found at Abbey Wood, Bexley, named after the Medieval Lesney Abbey. Whether the monks were using the plants for herbal medicine, another purpose (possibly as an adhesive), or for decorating the church on festival days is unknown.

Reports of daffodil poisoning occasionally occur, usually because daffodil bulbs have been mistaken for onions. Given the different appearance of the bulbs and the absence of the onion smell it is difficult to believe some of these. One well-attested example was in May 2009 when a number of schoolchildren fell ill at a primary school in Suffolk, England, after a daffodil bulb was added to soup during a cookery class. Symptoms of nausea, confusion, and abdominal pain may continue for several days.

A more serious problem is a skin irritation, or dermatitis, known as daffodil itch, which is something of an occupational hazard for professional pickers and florists. The skin can redden and become itchy, dry, and fissured, the result of calcium oxalate in the sap; this chemical compound is one of several toxins which daffodils have evolved to deter animals from eating them. Some cultivars are noted as being worse than others. Pickers as a consequence are encouraged to wear gloves.

A mid-Victorian British writer on daffodils mentions that there was a common belief at the time that the scent of daffodils is harmful, especially that of the most strongly fragrant: Tazettas and Jonquils. Headaches and even madness were said to be the result. Reactions to scent vary greatly between people, with some individuals claiming to physically suffer when exposed to certain strong smells. Often these are scents which others find utterly alluring, such as lilies, so a psychological rather than physical explanation may be more appropriate.

Wherever daffodils flourish they are often grown commercially, primarily for cut flowers. In Britain, Cornwall and Lincolnshire are the main growing areas. Often only a small proportion of the flowers are picked, which makes for spectacular scenes with flowers replacing the more usual arable crops to be found in fields. The range of varieties grown on this scale seems to be steadily increasing so the fields are by no means a uniform yellow, as can be seen in these Cornish ones.

Not just a flower
THE SYMBOLISM OF DAFFODILS

AS A SPRING FLOWER, it is no surprise that daffodils are seen as a symbol of rebirth and new life in many different cultures. In China what are called paperwhites in English (various forms of *Narcissus papyraceus*) are used to celebrate Spring Festival (New Year), the most important Chinese festival, around late January or early February. Traditionally, bulbs are grown without soil, set out on pebbles in shallow plates with their roots growing down into water in the bottom of the plate. In some cases, containers may be used to hold hundreds of bulbs. The plant is not native to China, but the practice is centuries old at least, and bulbs must originally have come from the Middle East along the Silk Road through central Asia. In those Asian cultures which celebrate the pre-Islamic spring festival of Nawroz, various spring flowers are used, with the Kurds of the Middle East using mostly the daffodil.

In western and central Europe, daffodils are often used to adorn churches as part of celebrations of spring and the resurrection of Christ. In Medieval Christian art, the flower is used as a symbol of paradise, and triumph over death; it is often associated with the Virgin Mary. In the Muslim Middle East it may, somewhat paradoxically, be seen as a symbol of death and planted on graves, because its growth in spring reminds people of the life to come. In classical Arabic poetry, Poeticus daffodils are seen as having "eyes" and therefore of being the eyes of the garden as well as being symbols of love, longing, and desire.

Daffodils have become the centres of festivals and festivities in some countries; in Newent, Gloucestershire, England, this can be seen as an active process as we shall see later. The Narzissenfest in the

Cultivated daffodils are descended from a small number of original species. There are, however, around thirty wild species to be found in southern Europe and the Maghreb (northwest Africa). Two are *Narcissus calcicola* **1** and *N. cordubensis* **2**, both from Spain. Over the last hundred years, some of these smaller species have been used in breeding new varieties, usually smaller plants for garden use, such as 'Itzim' **3**, bred from the rare Spanish species *N. cyclamineus* by American breeder Grant Mitsch (1982). Modern breeders are now working with a very wide range of genetic material derived from all wild species of *Narcissus*—the results will be seen in years to come as new varieties become available. ▶

small town of Altaussee in Styria, Austria, attracts thousands of people every year; indeed it is one of the biggest floral festivals in the country, although nowadays the role of the daffodil in this four-day festival in May seems to be more of an excuse for a civic celebration and general merrymaking than anything intrinsically floral or horticultural. The event involves the selection of a young woman as a "daffodil Queen," a parade with large floats, and a procession of boats on one of two local lakes, the boats supporting elaborate sculptures of cartoon-like animals often incorporating thousands of daffodil flowers.

Wales (or *Cymru* in Welsh) has a strong association with the daffodil, the flower being a national symbol. Unlike its original symbol, the dragon, which is of great antiquity (copied from Chinese silk imported during Roman times), the daffodil has represented the country for only about a century. It has been suggested that the reason for its becoming a national symbol is simply either confusion or fashion. The nation's original national plant was the leek (in Welsh, *cenhinen*), and the daffodil is often known as *cenhinen Pedr* (i.e., [St.] Peter's leek). The national day is St. David's Day (1 March, often seen as the first day of spring), and it has to be said that daffodils do make a more attractive emblem than a leek, especially when worn as a boutonnière. The widespread use of the flower as a national symbol probably dates back to the early twentieth century, when David Lloyd George, the first Welsh-born prime minister of the United Kingdom, started to wear it on St. David's Day; it was also used in ceremonies in 1911 to mark the investiture of the Prince of Wales at Caernarfon in north Wales.

Since the early 1990s, the daffodil has begun to acquire a new signification—that of hope for cancer patients. Promoted by the Marie Curie Cancer Care charity, the flower is used in the United Kingdom, in Ireland, and increasingly in other anglophone countries, as a symbol during the Great Daffodil Appeal, a fundraising week held early every March. In 2008, the charity had a new Jonquil named 'Marie Curie Diamond' to celebrate their Diamond Jubilee. The lesson perhaps is that traditions of symbolism are never static.

Reading a flower

THE DAFFODIL AS ROMANTIC EMBLEM

AS THE MOST COMMON and robust spring flower, the daffodil has inevitably become a symbol of the season, decorating any kind of merchandizing material which happens at this time of year, as well as decorations in churches and the garden and porch tableaux popular in the United States. This popular image of the daffodil as representing the force of nature in spring has been given an extra boost by the popularity of a poem by William Wordsworth, one of the best-known poets of both Great Britain and of the Romantic era as a whole.

> I wandered lonely as a Cloud
> That floats on high o'er Vales and Hills,
> When all at once I saw a crowd
> A host of dancing Daffodils;
> Along the Lake, beneath the trees,
> Ten thousand dancing in the breeze.
>
> The waves beside them danced, but
>   they
> Outdid the sparkling waves in glee:—
> A poet could not but be gay
> In such a laughing company:
> I gazed—and gazed—but little thought
> What wealth the show to me had
>   brought:

> For oft when on my couch I lie
> In vacant or in pensive mood,
> They flash upon that inward eye
> Which is the bliss of solitude,
> And then my heart with pleasure fills,
> And dances with the Daffodils.

The poem recalls 15 April 1802, on which day the poet and his sister Dorothy walked along the shore of Ullswater, in the English Lake District. Dorothy recorded in her journal how astounded they were by the numbers of the flower, mostly grouped but some scattered. The area is still famous for daffodils today.

The poem was published in 1807 as part of a collection (*Poems in Two Volumes*). A revised version was published in 1815. Over the years it has become one of the most famous poems in English and a national favourite in Britain, studied at school by children and endlessly quoted. The poem is now seen as one of the crucial texts of the Romantic Movement, which dominated north European culture during the late eighteenth and early nineteenth centuries. Romanticism started as a reaction to the early phases of industrialization and by extension to the Enlightenment, an earlier phase of European intellectual life which had stressed rationality. Romanticism stressed the personal experience, particularly the deep personal experience of nature or of emotion. The first line emphasizes the feeling of the individual; "lonely" at the time meant "alone" in a positive sense, not isolated, as it does now. The flowers are anthropomorphized—they dance and laugh, they are said to feel "glee," an emotion which is communicated to the poet (and presumably his sister too, although she is absent from the poem). This unity of feeling, between one part of creation and another, and of course with the artist, is a strong strand in Romantic thinking.

The Lake District itself later became one of the key sites of Victorian tourism, with the area around Lake Windermere filling with the summer villas of the wealthier middle classes. It was one of the most accessible areas of dramatic scenery to the main areas of manufacturing of the country, and the association of the area with the Romantic poets and Wordsworth's daffodils helped boost its popularity.

Like other pieces of great literature the poem has itself become a literary object, most notably in Jamaica Kincaid's 1990 novel *Lucy*. Kincaid herself is of Afro-Caribbean origin, and in *Lucy*, the heroine, a young woman in the Caribbean, recalls having to memorize the poem at school and feeling nothing for it, as daffodils do not grow in her homeland. The daffodils are a lightning rod for her intense feelings of alienation: she is seen as British and yet does not feel British. The poem and the flower therefore come to represent cultural imperialism in a writer noted for her post-colonial approach.

Kincaid, for her part, is fond of daffodils. A Caribbean blog noted in 2009 that she had over ten thousand in her garden and quoted her thus: "It dawned on me that it would look nice, and I wanted to vindicate Wordsworth . . . After all, it was not Wordsworth's fault that he was implicated in colonialism."

In an example of the growing and spreading power of the daffodil as a symbolic element in our culture, in 2004 the poem was read aloud by 150,000 schoolchildren across Britain, to celebrate the two hundredth anniversary of its writing, in an event organised by Marie Curie Cancer Care. In 2007, Cumbria Tourism attempted to gain a younger audience for the Lake District area by releasing a rap version, voiced by MC Nuts, a Lake District red squirrel. From the sublime to the ridiculous?

"Wild," but almost certainly naturalised, daffodils, by the shores of Ullswater, in the English Lake District. These, like nearly all the wild daffodils of the British Isles, are *Narcissus pseudonarcissus*.

1

Daffodil
Definitions

We all know what daffodils are, even though there may be some confusion as to where daffodils end and narcissus begin. Here, the intention is to take an overview of the broad categories of daffodil, mapping out the ground, so that we can make more sense of the flower's diversity. Before we start, we need to think about how daffodils reproduce and (by humans) get propagated.

Understanding a flower

DAFFODIL LIFE AND REPRODUCTION

LIKE ALL LIVING THINGS, daffodils are defined by their genes. Wild species spread themselves and their genes through seeds, and to a very limited extent by their bulbs dividing. The former is a sexual process, the result of an insect (usually a bee) visiting the flower, and involves a mixing of genes between parents, so that there is always at least some variation in the offspring. The latter is a vegetative, clonal process, so the daughter bulbs will be genetically identical to the parent.

Daffodil seed, like most bulb seed, is heavy. Which means that it does not travel on the wind like thistledown but instead falls near the parent plant. In nature, without occasional accidents, like landslides or floods, the rate of natural daffodil spread is slow. Commercial production is also relatively slow compared to that of many plants. Because daffodils sown from seed are so variable (the result of the lottery of sexual reproduction) the consistent production of a variety can only be achieved through the propagation of bulbs. Daffodils cannot be mass-produced from cuttings like many trees and shrubs, and even when the bulbs are skillfully divided the rate of increase is slow. Each new variety starts out as one bulb grown from one seed, and so all the plants of one named variety are genetically identical, members of a clone. At least that is the situation now. In the early days of daffodil breeding, a variety name might be given to all the bulbs derived from seedlings grown from the same seedpod, which were not all identical. As well in early days, demand for a new variety occasionally outstripped supply, and so very similar plants might be substituted; this is possibly the case with the well-known 'King Alfred' (1899): heritage daffodil specialists now do not know which of several clones is the real monarch.

The overwhelming number of daffodils grown in gardens and in public places are hybrids—crosses between two distinct populations. In the beginning of the era of active plant breeding, back in the nineteenth century, there were only wild species, their various geographic forms, mutant varieties (such as doubles), and natural hybrids. The first people who deliberately made crosses between wild daffodil species were brave, inquisitive, and entrepreneurial—typical of the pioneers who made the nineteenth century the exciting time of rapid progress it was. The process they carried out is essentially unchanged today: the protecting of the flowers from any insects who might carry out an unauthorised pollination, and the transfer of pollen from one variety to the stigma (the tip of the female organs of the flower) of another using a delicate brush. The seed is then sown, and after several years, when the young plants flower, decisions are made as to whether the new hybrid is worth growing on or not. Usually not: of the thousands of seedlings raised, very few are worthy of further selection.

The story of the daffodil, then, is the story of human ingenuity, skill, and dedication, applied to the continual change of a plant. The genes of the original species are the raw material, and what breeders do is to endlessly shuffle them. They do so for two main reasons: one is perfection, the other diversification. Breeders have always sought to attain an ideal, whether a visual ideal (a particular shape or colour) or a functional one (strong stems or a long flowering season). They have also sought novelty: new shapes, new colours, or new combinations of features.

The genus *Narcissus* is one of some sixty in the family Amaryllidaceae, which also includes snowdrops, clivia, and of course *Amaryllis*. What sets *Narcissus* apart is the cup or corona. The standard pattern for flowers is for them to be made up of four whorls of tissue: sepals (which often form the protective bud), petals, stamens (carrying male pollen-bearing organs), and carpels (protecting the female organ). Many flowers, including tulips, lilies, and daffodils, have sepals which are practically identical to and function as petals—together the sepals and petals are called the perianth, the individual petal-like structures perianth segments. Debate among botanists has raged since the middle of the nineteenth century about whether the corona is derived from the stamens or the perianth segments; similar structures can be seen in other members of the amaryllis family, although it is thought that they arose independently. Now, it appears as if the question has been solved—the daffodil cup is a structure that has evolved independently of either perianth segments or stamens and is unique to the daffodil. What evolutionary advantage it serves remains open to question—possibly it helps directs pollinating insects or protects the stamens from rain.

There are some seventy species of *Narcissus*, although some botanists might reduce this to fifty, and others increase to a hundred. As with many plant genera, there are a few species spread over a large area and a "centre of diversity," where a small area includes a much larger number of localised species. For the daffodil, that centre of diversity is the mountains of the Iberian peninsula (i.e., Spain and Portugal) and the mountains just across the water in the Maghreb (i.e., Morocco and Algeria). Only one species, *N. pseudonarcissus*, has a really wide distribution in western Europe; *N. poeticus* (the familiar pheasant's eye) and the white *N. serotinus* are found across the regions immediately north of the Mediterranean, while the heavily fragrant white *N. tazetta* is found further eastwards around the Mediterranean into Iran.

Key to understanding daffodils and how they came to be an important garden flower is to see them in the context of their geography and climate. As so often, it helps to compare and contrast with tulips. The tulip centre of diversity is in central Asia, an extreme continental climate where winters are long and cold and summers hot and dry; tulips have evolved to make the most of a very short spring growing season. Daffodils by contrast enjoy a western Mediterranean climate where a long cool (but not cold) moist winter is followed by a spring with reasonable soil moisture levels—the result is a long growing season; dormancy begins only with the summer drought. Compared to the tulip, the daffodil year is a languid one; many start to make root growth in late summer, and their leaves may stay green until early summer the next year.

North of the western Mediterranean climate zone is the Atlantic zone, where prevailing westerly winds bring rain and temperatures moderated by blowing in from over a vast body of water. Visitors to Cornwall or Ireland will be familiar with the feeling that sometimes it is difficult to tell whether it is December or June; while a Chinese friend living in Edinburgh once said to me, "Every day here is like autumn." Moving eastwards, the Atlantic climate zone develops a clearer distinction between winter and summer in eastern England, into northeastern France, the Netherlands, and Denmark, but certain factors remain: rainfall which is relatively predictable on an annual basis, cool summers, mild winters, and long springs.

Not missing their summer drought (which tulips need to stimulate flower bud formation), the daffodils of the western Mediterranean hills are in heaven in the Atlantic climate zone— their roots can grow into moist soil from mid-summer, they can push their shoots up above the earth during mild phases in the winter, and then flower in a spring that goes on for months. Both for daffodils and for us, the long drawn-out, on-and-off springs of the Atlantic zone are one of its joys. For gardeners or simply people who enjoy daffodils in public spaces and in other people's gardens, long springs allow a succession of varieties to flower and finish flowering in their own time, and not be scorched to a premature end. Gardeners in continental climates in contrast (such as the American Midwest) often experience a concertina'd spring with spring and early summer flowers all performing together, and all over too quickly.

Bringing order

THE DIVISIONS

ALL WILD DAFFODIL species have now been used by daffodil breeders to produce the approximately twenty-seven thousand registered varieties, although the vast majority of garden and florist varieties are derived from genes from a limited number of species. Such a vast number of varieties needs order. Over the years various schemes of classifying daffodils have been proposed, of which the one set out by the Daffodil Committee of the RHS in 1950 has lasted the course of time, with minor modifications. It is a mixture of classification on the basis of plant form and on genetic origin. Here, we will run through the divisions, in the process getting to know the basic outline of this beautiful and fascinating group of plants. Divisions will then be referred to through the rest of the book with a capital letter (e.g., Trumpets, Jonquils). However, anyone who wishes to pass with the daffodil community will need to learn to refer to the divisions by number.

The average garden daffodil has a big yellow flower with a big trumpet. 'King Alfred' (John Kendall, UK, 1899) is the best known and is everybody's idea of a typical daffodil. It is derived from an Iberian species, *Narcissus hispanicus*, and if anything deserves the title of "ur-daffodil," it is this. *Narcissus hispanicus* is a splendid plant, sturdy, richly coloured, early, and free-flowering. Only its distinctive perianth segments mark it out, as they are narrow and twisted—elegant but unlike the solid background for the trumpet we are used to. 'King Alfred' is a good example of **DIVISION ONE—TRUMPET DAFFODILS**, where each stem has a single flower where the length of the cup (i.e., the trumpet) is greater than or equal to the length of the perianth segments.

Any cursory look at a collection of daffodils or at the pictures above the sale bins in a garden centre shows that there is a great deal of variation: there are white flowers and pale flowers, wide trumpets, narrow trumpets, trumpets which flare out a bit, and trumpets which veer towards orange, or even red-orange. There is often a difference in colour between the perianth segments and the cup (i.e., the trumpet)—these are referred to as bicolours, and it seems to be the general pattern that the cup is a richer yellow than the perianth segments. Except that there are some where the cup is paler than the perianth segments—these are known as reverse bicolours.

Other species have contributed to the Trumpet genepool, apart from *Narcissus hispanicus*. Not surprisingly, one is the widespread west European *N. pseudonarcissus*, a hardy and robust little plant, with a trumpet which is considerably

Trumpet daffodils began with *Narcissus hispanicus* **1** although the genes of other species are now well blended in. 'King Alfred' **2** is typical. 'Apricot' (de Graaff Bros., Netherlands, 1897) **3** is a good example of an older variety—notice the thin and twisted perianth segments, which would be utterly unacceptable among show judges and therefore most modern breeders. 'American Heritage' (Elise and Richard Havens, USA, 1993) **4** is a good example of modern breeding—notice the flat and even perianth segments.

Large-cupped daffodils show a great deal of variety. 'Chy Noweth' (2003) **1** is a modern take by Ron Scamp on what most would see as the classic daffodil. 'Golden Amber' (Ballydorn Bulb Farm, Northern Ireland, 1975) **2**, 'May Muriel' (J. J. Grullemans & Sons, Netherlands, 1957) **3**, and 'Edge Grove' (Carncairn Daffodils, Northern Ireland, 1990) **4** are good examples of modern varieties. 'Kernow' (Ron Scamp, UK, 1993) **5**, a reverse bicolour from the leading Cornish breeder, celebrates the county's name in its ancestral language, 'Sheviok' (Tom Bloomer, Northern Ireland, 1987) **6** is late and, unlike many older orange-cupped varieties, sunproof. 'Marlborough' (Ron Scamp, 1991) **7** is a pink-cupped variety.

longer in proportion to the rest of the flower than we expect from cultivated plants.

In **DIVISION TWO—LARGE-CUPPED DAFFODILS**, the length of the cup is more than a third as long as the length of the perianth segments but less than equal to it. It is the largest division, some forty-five percent of those registered by the Royal Horticultural Society. They originated in crosses between the Trumpet species (such as *Narcissus hispanicus*) and *N. poeticus* and other similar species with only a very shallow cup, crosses made by those who were the very first conscious breeders. The same type of combination of character and colour seen in the Trumpets can be seen here, although there is a definite tendency towards orange-red cups, which can be particularly spectacular set against pale or white perianth segments. This cup colouring is derived from the intense orange of the very diminutive Poeticus

Small-cupped daffodils all do tend to look similar to the uninitiated. 'Doctor Hugh' (Brian Duncan, Northern Ireland, 1975) **1**, 'My Sweetheart' (John Reed, USA, 1997) **2**, 'Gorran' (Ron Scamp, 1986) **3**, and 'John's Delight' (Ron Scamp, 1995) **4** are all typical, in being mid to late season and relatively tall.

cup. Starting with 'Mrs. R. O. Backhouse' (pre-1921), pink-cupped flowers have also been an important part of the development of varieties in the Large-cupped division. Most successful of all, and arguably the most successful daffodil of all time in sheer biomass distributed around the world, has been all-yellow 'Carlton' (pre-1927), which brings spring to countless parks and roadsides as well as gardens.

'Carlton' is instructive—to most of us it looks like a "typical" daffodil, i.e., a member of the Trumpet division. But get out a ruler and by a matter of millimetres it counts as Large-cupped. This is one reason why this division is so large—it is partly a matter of definition. The other factor is a genetic one, as there is such a rich source of material to choose from.

DIVISION THREE—SMALL-CUPPED DAFFODILS have cups less than one-third the length of the perianth segments. They show the influence of *Narcissus poeticus* and allied species even more strongly, so there is a strong tendency for strongly coloured but modest-sized cups and white or pale perianth segments. "Rimmed" varieties are those where the outer edge of the cup is flared outwards, and may or may not be distinctly coloured.

All double daffodils are grouped into **DIVISION FOUR—DOUBLES**. Feelings about these are inevitably mixed; a lot of people do not like double flowers, whereas some who find double roses acceptable and even desirable feel that double daffodils are somehow not the real thing. There is nothing new about

Doubles vary enormously in their form, as do reactions to them. Old doubles like the rare 'Feu de Joie' (William Copeland, UK, pre-1927) **1** tend to be untidy, in contrast to the elegant arrangement of 'Crackington' AGM (David Lloyd, UK, 1986) **2**. 'White Lion' AGM (de Graaff-Gerharda, Netherlands, pre-1949) **3** represents an intermediate stage. 'Wave' (unknown, Netherlands, 2004) **4** is an oddity—the corona is doubled up, but not the perianth segments. 'Glowing Red' (K. J. Heazlewood, Australia, 1968) **5** might find more universal favour. 'Golden Bear' (Brian Duncan, 1992) **6** may be attractive to some but looks a mutant to others. 'Abba' AGM (J. M. van Dijk, Netherlands, 1984) **7** will offend few, especially as this is a multi-headed Tazetta with a spicy scent, ideal for early flowering indoors. ▶

them—Vincent Sion, a Fleming who came to live in London in the early seventeenth century, introduced a double which became known as 'Double Van Sion', but as with many old varieties it acquired several other names over time (it is now synonymous with 'Telamonius Plenus'). It and other doubles of great antiquity are vigorous plants and can form large colonies over time in old gardens. 'Eggs and Bacon' is another, a *Narcissus pseudonarcissus* × *N. poeticus* cross that has been around since the early eighteenth century; it is now called 'Orange Phoenix'.

Most of these early doubles have a somewhat messy appearance—lots of perianth segments or petaloids (mutated floral parts which function as and resemble petals) packed into a bunch, looking very much the mutants that they are. The truth is that they are curiosities which suddenly appeared and which were grown on and propagated because they are out-of-the-ordinary. Conscious breeding of doubles aims at flowers that have elegantly arranged perianth segments, or perianth segments, often in two different colours, which are bundled together in an attractive way.

'Rosedown' is a Triandrus, a hybrid between *Narcissus triandrus* and a Large-cupped daffodil, raised during the 1940s by Alec Gray, a Cornish breeder who specialised in dwarf varieties—classed as those with a maximum height of 30cm (1 foot).

In casting our eye from Division Four to **DIVISION FIVE—TRIANDRUS**, we have crossed a watershed. No longer are we among the familiar daffodils of the florist or the public park, but among plants which are generally smaller, with differently proportioned flowers, and sometimes with more than one flower to a head. These are the flowers which many people are happier calling "narcissus," although the connoisseurs like to call them "the upper divisions." Triandrus daffodils are descended from the Iberian *Narcissus triandrus*, with a distinct bell-shaped cup, and usually with at least two flowers per stem. With their downward-pointing flowers, they have a distinctly modest appearance and tend to be seen as delicate and pretty rather than showy. The species and the early hybrids have a reputation for being short-lived (which is an inherent factor) and being a bit fussier about soils than others (they like acidic, moist ones). From early on, most Triandrus varieties were hybrids between the species and daffodils from other divisions, and over time the longevity of the division has improved.

DIVISION SIX—CYCLAMINEUS, descended from Iberian *Narcissus*

Narcissus cyclamineus **1** is a rare species from damp woodland in Spain. Its early flowering, diminutive size, and swept-back perianth segments have been handed down to its descendants. 'Charity May' (Cyril Coleman, UK, pre-1948) **2** and 'Mite' AGM (Josslyn A. R. Gore-Booth, Ireland, 1965) **3** clearly show their ancestry. 'Jenny' AGM (Cyril Coleman, pre-1943) **4**, 'Dove Wings' AGM (Cyril Coleman, pre-1949) **5**, and 'Kaydee' AGM (Brian Duncan, 1984) **6** are less obvious descendants.

cyclamineus are slightly more conventional, with miniature trumpets, one to a stem. What makes them stand out is the way the perianth segments are slightly bent back, reminiscent of cyclamen, giving them an appearance either of being windswept or surprised. The Cyclamineus division gives us many durable, early-flowering, and generally smaller-sized plants.

So far, we have met only minimal fragrance; but in **DIVISION SEVEN— JONQUILS** we meet it as part of a defining characteristic. Whereas the last two divisions are based on species with a history in cultivation going back only to the nineteenth century, the Jonquils have been known and loved since the seventeenth century at least. Often with three flowers to a stem, and narrow rush-like leaves, they look distinct. Descended from Narcissus jonquilla, these are tough plants, with a reputation for disease resistance. However, crosses between them and other divisions are often sterile, which has reduced their influence in breeding. They have a particular association with the American South.

Scent goes up another order of magnitude in **DIVISION EIGHT—TAZETTAS**, sometimes almost to the point of being overpowering. Tazettas tend to have multiple flowers atop tall stems, with an

A selection of Jonquils. 'Katherine Jenkins' (2007) **1**, named for a Welsh singer, is the result of a cross between a non-Jonquil and *Narcissus jonquilla;* its breeder Ron Scamp of Cornwall has tried this approach to breeding Jonquils with several other successful results, such as 'An-Gof' (1999) **2** and 'Little Meg' (2008) **3**. 'Sailboat' AGM (1980) **4** and 'Intrigue' AGM (1970) **5** are from one of the best American breeders, William G. Pannill. 'Intrigue' is among the most popular reverse bicolours. 'Bunting' AGM (1975) is from the great American breeder Grant Mitsch **6**.

overall appearance of just waiting to be picked. Most flower in mid to late season. With a wide natural distribution around the Mediterranean, these were the first daffodils to be taken into cultivation, from where trade routes took them as far as Japan many centuries ago. They are inclined to be tender and need hot summers to encourage repeat flowering. An early attempt to produce hardier plants for northern winters were the Poetaz types, hybrids between Tazettas and the Poeticus division made in the Netherlands in the late nineteenth century.

DIVISION NINE—POETICUS are derived from a group of closely related species common to the countries on the northern shores of the Mediterranean. The cup is very shallow and often brightly coloured, so the overall impression is of flat white perianth segments with a central ring. Being common, readily available, and easy to grow, the original species were used very early in the history of daffodil hybridisation. These have a strong tendency to be tall and late flowering.

Plants derived from *Narcissus bulbocodium*, known by its Victorian name of hoop petticoat daffodil (who these days knows what a hoop petticoat is, let alone wears one?) make up **DIVISION TEN—BULBOCODIUM**. This is a relatively

The super-fragrant Tazettas. *Narcissus papyraceus* **1**, commonly known as paperwhite, flowers very, very early but is suitable for growing outdoors only in mild climates. 'Laurens Koster' (pre-1906) **2** was bred by Albert Vis of the Netherlands; 'Dan du Plessis' (1996) **3**, bred at the government-funded Rosewarne research station in Cornwall, commemorates one of the county's great daffodil men.

Poeticus all look very similar, and indeed many might question whether any variety, old or new, is an improvement on the original species. These three are all old attempts: 'Sarchedon' (Engleheart, pre-1910) **1**, 'Actaea' AGM (G. Lubbe & Son, Netherlands, pre-1919) **2**, and 'Ornatus' (James Walker, UK, selected from an old French variety, pre-1860) **3**.

The original *Narcissus bulbocodium.*

'Valdrome' (1965) **1**, bred by the Dutch company of J. Gerritsen & Son, who were pioneers in producing Split-coronas, and Ron Scamp's 'Jack Wood' (1965) **2** are two of a varied and growing division.

The complex ancestry of the dwarf 'Toto' (William Pannill, 1983) is typical of Division Twelve, where no one particular species' genes dominates. It is a cross between *Narcissus jonquilla* and 'Jenny', which is a cross between *N. cyclamineus* and 'Mitylene'—an Engleheart cross between an unknown Small-cupped seedling and 'Beacon' (Engleheart again); that being the result of mating a cross between two different wild Poeticus forms with 'Princess Mary'—a Leeds hybrid between *N. pseudonarcissus* × *N. poeticus* and simple *N. poeticus*.

new division, as extensive breeding here is recent. Natives of the Maghreb and Iberian Peninsula, the Bulbocodiums are quite unlike other daffodils, with minimal perianth segments and a greatly expanded cup. There is a very high level of variation, and there is the possibility that this is the most "advanced" daffodil, currently in an active state of evolution. Although often grown by specialists as an alpine houseplant, many forms thrive in damp but well-drained ground and can even naturalise in lawns. Given the level of recent breeding, this is clearly a division to keep an eye on.

Also the focus of much recent breeding has been **DIVISION ELEVEN—SPLIT-CORONA**, sometimes known as Split-cupped daffodils (and often by other very uncomplimentary names). This is the most controversial division,

with many people hating the very idea of the cup being splayed out to become what is functionally another layer of perianth segments. They are popular with florists, and many breeders, who have led an otherwise blameless life working with other divisions, seem to find it hard to resist breeding yet more.

My personal prediction is that **DIVISION TWELVE—MISCELLANEOUS** will be the one to grow most dramatically in future years. Hybrids made across species and division boundaries, often with the help of biotechnology, will undoubtedly increase the number of varieties here. Although there have been a few since the early days of hybridisation, it is only in the last few decades that numbers have begun to escalate. A sign of the future is surely 'Tête-à-Tête', bred by Alec Gray and registered in 1949, one of the most popular daffodils of recent times, with genes from Cyclamineus, Poeticus, and Tazetta varieties.

DIVISION THIRTEEN—NATURAL SPECIES, VARIANTS, AND HYBRIDS covers all the wild species, their natural forms, and naturally occurring hybrids. This is primarily territory for enthusiasts, as many of the natural species are fussy in their cultivation requirements. There are some oddities, such as *Narcissus cavanillesii* with its minimal, almost microscopic cup, so making it look utterly unlike other daffodils, and the green, autumn-flowering *N. viridiflorus*.

Finally, **MINIATURES** are not a class on their own, as small-flowered or small-stature plants can be found among all divisions. Many wild species are small, and growers of alpines have always grown a certain amount of miniature daffodils. Recently, however, the general public has started to appreciate small-growing plants, partly because of the need for varieties to grow in confined urban spaces (there is a similar trend towards small vegetable varieties). Breeders are very much responding to this.

The pioneer breeder of miniatures was Alec Gray (1895–1986), whose 'Tête-à-Tête' was a stimulant for more breeding of small varieties. Wild species are the source of much of this new diversity, both rarities from the mountains of Spain and the familiar *Narcissus pseudonarcissus*. There are a few miniature Trumpets, and many more Bulbocodiums, Cyclamineus, Triandrus, and Jonquils, but very few Tazettas or Poeticus—the tall flower stem is very difficult to breed out.

Fragrance varies greatly between daffodil varieties, although there is a strong relationship with original species. Trumpets and some Large-cupped have a faint scent. Many Large-cupped and Small-cupped have little, while Triandrus and Cyclamineus varieties are totally scentless. Jonquils are famously fragrant, with a clear sweet scent. Tazettas are fabulously fragrant, but to the extent that they can be overpowering. Poeticus varieties are also often good, with a moderately strong sweet scent.

For those who find the complex craftsmanship of hybridisation all too much and prefer the simple, and often diminutive beauty of the original species, patience and attention to detail are required as many are demanding in the conditions they need to give of their best. *Narcissus fernandesii* var. *cordubensis* **1** and *N. willkommii* **2** are among many species found growing in the mountains of southern Spain and Portugal.

From the Tombs of the Pharaohs

EARLY DAFFODIL HISTORY

White Tazetta daffodils are known from the tombs of ancient Egypt, and one of the greatest of the Pharaohs, Ramses II, was buried with daffodil bulbs placed on his eyes. Occasional mentions are to be found in classical texts, and the plants are known to have been grown by the Byzantines, whose Orthodox Christian empire dominated the eastern Mediterranean in the period following the collapse of the Roman Empire in 476.

The Byzantines were succeeded ultimately by the Ottoman Empire, founded originally by Turkish-speaking nomads from central Asia who, after a few centuries of settling down, began to take gardening and flower culture very seriously. They are known primarily for their love of the tulip, and it was through them that Europe acquired its first bulbs of this flower, but they also cultivated several daffodil varieties, which were also traded into Christian Europe.

A remarkable book, published in 1613, gives us a good insight into the status of the daffodil as a garden ornamental at a time just before the almost exponential changes of the Enlightenment and the Industrial Revolution altered the world forever. *Hortus Eystettensis* was commissioned by Prince-Bishop Johann Conrad von Gemmingen (1561–1612) of the southern German city of Eichstätt, as an illustration of the collection of plants which had been gathered together in the castle garden. What makes von Gemmingen's garden and book special is that for the first time in western history, plants are being collected and celebrated not for their use, but for their own inherent interest. Forty daffodil varieties are illustrated, although the distinctions between them are not made at all clear. *Narcissus pseudonarcissus*, *N. poeticus*, *N. minor*, and *N. bulbocodium* are shown, several Jonquil and Tazetta types, two interspecies hybrids, and six doubles. The hybrids are *N. ×incomparabilis*—a hybrid between *N. pseudonarcissus* and *N. poeticus*, the two most common European species, and *N. ×medioluteus*—a

hybrid of *N. poeticus* and *N. tazetta*. John Parkinson (1567–1650), an English herbalist and botanist of the same period, is said to have mentioned seventy-eight daffodil varieties, although it is even less clear than with *Hortus Eystettensis* what distinctions were made between them.

The numbers of varieties slowly and haphazardly increased over time. It is important for us looking back into history to understand that well into the nineteenth century, the concept of species crossing was an alien one. There was no idea that new varieties or species could arise through human intervention—this would have seemed the work of magic, and quite possibly of blasphemy. A few insightful early scientists, such as Linnaeus (1707–1778), and a small number of nurserymen had begun to carry out experiments with hybridisation, but with daffodils there was a drawback—the five years or so it took the plants to flower from seed. The gardener John Rea (d. 1681), who was reputed to have the largest collection of tulips in England, wrote instructions for raising daffodils from seed, but few followed his advice.

Three old daffodil varieties. 'Sulphur Phoenix' **1** is of unknown origin, eighteenth century at least; a robust plant capable of surviving many years in old gardens; also known as 'Codlings and Cream'—codlings referring to small apples used for cooking. 'Rip van Winkle' **2** is an early-flowering double of obscure Irish origin, first recorded in 1884; double varieties like this would have been picked out by our gardening ancestors for their novelty value. 'Sir Watkin' **3** was raised, or selected, by W. Pickstone in England in the late nineteenth century.

Chance hybridisation by the bees (and the even smaller chance that seedlings which resulted from such crosses would survive five years of garden weeding) would be the only way that new varieties would occur. We have to imagine a gardener of the time looking around at their flowers in springtime and suddenly noticing, among the established clumps of the familiar, something new—a flower with a different shape, colour, or combination of parts. They would then have to ensure that the plant was cared for, that it built up a clump over time, and that it was then dug up and divided and the bulbs distributed. It might go to some other gardeners, and then be brought to the notice of one of the really small number of people with the leisure and interest to pursue such things—if this happened, then it might then be given a name and distributed further.

The names of early daffodils can cause immense confusion. We have to remember that there was no concept of the species as distinct to garden varieties or hybrids, and no understanding of the importance of having just one name, and making sure that plants distributed kept that name. Bulbs, so easy to store, and to trade over long distances, would lose names, and gain names, with remarkable rapidity.

A remarkable insight into daffodil origins has been made by Spanish researchers who analysed illustrations of daffodils in books published in Europe from the sixteenth century on—it was from this time that plants were depicted with a usable level of accuracy. They concluded that some Iberian species can be identified in illustrations of the seventeenth and early eighteenth centuries, showing that these were in cultivation in central and northern European gardens at this time. However, certain other species also appear but lack later records; they concluded that these more southerly species were possibly less hardy and so died out. Indeed both Parkinson and Philip Miller (1691–1771), another important writer on gardens of the time, mentioned that imported Spanish bulbs often died out after a few years. On the basis of this study, we can be fairly certain that white daffodils had several different points of origin, having originated more than once in separate species. It also appears that doubles too originated separately on multiple occasions from different original species.

A clerical breakthrough

WILLIAM HERBERT

It is desirable to call the attention of the humblest cultivators, of every labourer indeed, or operative, who has a spot of garden, or a ledge at his window, to the infinite variety of Narcissi that may be thus raised, and most easily in pots at his window, if not exposed too much to sun and wind, offering him a source of harmless and interesting amusement, and perhaps a little profit and celebrity.

These were the words of William Herbert (1778–1847), writing in 1843. An Oxford-educated member of the gentry, he entered Parliament, and then the Church, finally becoming The Very Reverend Dean of Manchester in the Church of England. One of that famous eighteenth- and nineteenth-century English type, "the hunting parson," he was reportedly fond of outdoor life and sport, as well as being a poet and a keen amateur naturalist—as were so many of his clerical colleagues. He did some experimental breeding, mostly with florist's flowers (e.g., auriculas and polyanthus) but also with some agricultural plants, notably swede (rutabaga) and other fodder crops. This was at a time when early scientists or gentlemen-experimenters like himself were first systematically making hybrids between plant species.

Very often the hybrids turned out to be sterile, which confirmed the sneaking suspicion of many that God had created nature, and it was not the job of Man to meddle and try to improve on His creation. Herbert, however, discovered that some of his hybrids were fertile, which led him to challenge the concept of the species as being fixed and immutable. This led him to wonder whether the species was actually rather an arbitrary and artificial distinction.

These were radical thoughts for anyone in early nineteenth-century Europe, especially for a member of the established church. Herbert decided to carry out an experiment, and it was daffodils which he chose as his subject. He was interested in the family into which the daffodil had been classified, the Amaryllidaceae, and in writing the first study of the family he dissected the flowers of all 150 daffodil varieties then known in Britain, in order to develop a classification system. While working as a country vicar in Yorkshire, he began to suspect that some daffodil varieties were hybrids—partly because many were sterile. Moreover he thought the same about some he had found growing wild while travelling in France. Working very

much as a scientist, setting up a hypothesis (that some naturally occurring daffodil species are hybrids), he sought to test it, by making crosses himself, to see if the new plants resembled either their parents or his suspected wild hybrids. His hunch turned out to be right, and some of the wild plants did appear to be natural hybrids. From this he concluded that it would be possible to deliberately make crosses between daffodils in order to generate new ornamental varieties. Hence the quotation at the head of this section; it was not unusual for Victorian garden writers to evangelize about the ease, pleasure, and possible profit of making new plant varieties.

Shortly before his death, Herbert published a paper on hybridisation which in many ways was very advanced for its time, suggesting (on the evidence of nearly forty years of experimentation) that hybridisation and speciation had considerably diversified the Almighty's original creation of the Plant Kingdom. Not only this, but he also suggested a

model of possible continual development, many years before Charles Darwin's Theory of Evolution. While his scientific ideas did not make a major impact, his 1837 book, *Amaryllidaceae*, helped to stimulate daffodil breeding, and almost certainly inspired the three pioneers of systematic selection and breeding: Edward Leeds, William Backhouse, and Peter Barr.

William Herbert was not only one of the fathers of modern plant breeding, but his example was useful in the battle to get hybridisation accepted in Victorian Britain. Much like genetic modification is seen by some today as "unnatural" and therefore dangerous or even immoral, there was a certain level of opposition to hybridisation during this period. The fact that William Herbert, a Dean of the Church of England, had not only carried it out, but recommended it to others, was made great use of by progressives within the horticultural community.

Another selection of historic daffodils. 'Mary Copeland' (Double, pre-1914) **1** and 'Irene Copeland' (Double, pre-1915) **2** were raised by William Copeland, who was responsible for about forty varieties in the early twentieth century. 'Horsfieldii' (pre-1845) **3** is a dwarf Trumpet, named for its breeder, John Horsfield. 'Sweetness' AGM (R. V. Favell, UK) **4**, a sweetly-scented Jonquil of the 1930s, represents the growing interest at this time in less "conventional" varieties.

A mysterious pioneer
EDWARD LEEDS

EDWARD LEEDS (1802–1877) played a crucial role in early daffodil breeding but remains a somewhat elusive character, with little known about him. Daffodil growers who followed him were in no doubt as to the scale of his achievements; this can be seen from the fact that one of the early attempts at classifying daffodils had a section named after him—Leedsii.

Leeds came from a family of small-scale Manchester manufacturers; he became a stockbroker but was by no means a wealthy man. It is possible that he had a short-lived nursery business, but he appears to have been more of a gentleman-amateur. Some of his horticultural interests were very much in tune with the times—in particular the growing-on of seed of exotics from lands being newly explored. Herbert published his article on new daffodil varieties in 1843; and Leeds's publication of pictures of some of his hybrids in 1851 (to accompany an article in *The Gardeners' Magazine of Botany*) indicates that he was following the learned cleric's advice. In his article, Leeds explained some of the basics of how he made daffodil crosses, including bringing later-flowering species inside the house to persuade them to flower at the same time as early-flowering ones, so he could cross-pollinate them. One particular Leeds achievement was his creation of a range of pale hybrids, using garden and wild hybrids involving *Narcissus poeticus*. Daffodils would no longer be dominated by rich yellow.

One of our few sources on Leeds's life was William Brockbank, a Manchester surveyor and well-known local gardener, who never met him but was so fascinated by his reputation that he went to visit his old garden, to find out what he could and write about him. He described Leeds as having "rummaged Europe for Narcissi for his garden. Every nurseryman's catalogue was looked over, and every variety obtained that he could hear of." The old garden was "quite hidden from view from the road by huge overgrown Rhododendrons, Box and Laurels, 15 to 20 feet high. . . . the garden was ablaze with Daffodils—growing by thousands, almost wild."

Failing health, and, it would appear, a lack of interest from the public in his daffodils, led Leeds to lose interest later in life. Brockbank recorded, "He was much annoyed, and reasonably so, at the want of appreciation on the part of the floricultural world for his seedling Daffodils . . . . [H]e had almost made up his mind to dig a hole and bury the bulbs out of sight." This early, and probably very rich seam of genetic diversity was saved, however, as word had spread that

Leeds was considering giving up; and in 1874 nurseryman Peter Barr organised a syndicate to buy Leeds's collection of around twenty-four thousand bulbs for £100 (£7,240 at today's prices).

For many years Leeds varieties were lost to commerce, but heirloom daffodil collectors and growers Kate and Duncan Donald have now rescued several and made them available once again. Among them the Large-cupped 'Frank Miles' (pre-1877), which their catalogue notes as "a fitting daffodil to be named after the tall and elegant artist, architect, keen plantsman and friend of Oscar Wilde," its open star-like shape very typical of older varieties and quite unlike modern ones.

Botany in the genes
THE BACKHOUSE FAMILY

THE BACKHOUSES were almost a botanical dynasty. Their activities as amateur naturalists and plant breeders, and the later involvement of some of them in professional botany and crop improvement, was made possible by a successful family banking business, founded by Edward Backhouse (1781–1860) in Sunderland in the north of England. Like many enlightened business people of the period, the family were Quakers. William Backhouse (1779–1844), Edward's brother, was a well-known naturalist from nearby Durham, and his son, also William (1807–1869), engaged in daffodil breeding, among many other country pursuits. Starting in 1856, this younger Backhouse worked on colour, initially using Poeticus varieties and moving on to *Narcissus pseudonarcissus*; he is also credited with starting a group of hybrids that were developed much further by Peter Barr, who took over his collection of daffodils shortly before his death. We might wonder what his son, Robert Ormston Backhouse (1854–1940), came to think of this handover of the family silver, as Robert went on to become the most prolific daffodil breeder of the family.

The Backhouses were undoubtedly good breeders, but they were also good at marketing, which is often more important. Whereas Herbert and Leeds seedlings had unmemorable latinate names (e.g., Herbert's 'Spofforthiae Spurius'), the Backhouses were more likely to use names with selling power; two of their most successful were 'Emperor' and 'Empress' (both pre-1869 Trumpets derived from *Narcissus bicolor* × *N. pseudonarcissus*). They also promoted the idea of using daffodils in the house in pots to provide early season colour.

To be fair, and accurate, Robert Backhouse's breeding work was shared with

Old glasshouses for apricots and other tender fruits await restoration at Sutton Court, Herefordshire, the property which has been in the Backhouse family for generations; daffodils which were once part of a breeding programme have survived and spread over many years **1**. 'Little Witch' (Cyclamineus, pre-1921), a Sarah Backhouse hybrid, with *Fritillaria meleagris* **2**; 'Bittern' (Miscellaneous, 1921) **3**, another Sarah Backhouse hybrid. 'Empress' (Trumpet, pre-1869) **4** and 'C. J. Backhouse' (Large-cupped, pre-1869) **5**, both William Backhouse plants, and also by him, 'Mrs. Langtry' (Large-cupped, pre-1869) **6**; Mrs. Langtry was a British musical hall singer and high-society courtesan. 'Conspicuus' (Small-cupped, pre-1869) **7** and 'Niveth' (Triandrus, 1932) **8** are both by Henry Backhouse, Robert's brother. The double 'Glowing Phoenix' (pre-1930) **9** is by Robert Backhouse. ▶

his wife, Sarah Elizabeth (1857–1921)—indeed in some ways she appeared to have been the driving force in their daffodil breeding. The couple lived in Herefordshire, near the Welsh border, and lived the life of country gentry "of independent means"—i.e., they did not need to work but lived that very Victorian life which mixed country pursuits (hunting and archery) with amateur science: photography and plant and animal breeding (daffodils, lilies, and cats). Daffodils were the real passion however. Sarah first won an award from the RHS for 'Moonbeam', a pure white, in 1901 and was awarded the Peter Barr Memorial Cup for her hybridising work in 1916. She raised many highly praised varieties and was particularly focussed on those daffodils whose flowers had a white perianth and red corona.

Two years after her death, Robert named 'Mrs. R. O. Backhouse' for her and launched it on the world. This was the first pink-cup daffodil. It was a worthy memorial for someone who had undoubtedly been a gifted breeder, and one of the first women to really make a mark in any field of plant breeding. In an obituary in *The Garden* magazine of 19 February 1921, it was said of her: "Few of the famous raisers of new varieties were less known on committees or at meetings, and it was not very often that she staged many flowers in public, but when she did, it was something like a revelation to see what was there."

Yet another generation of the Backhouses worked as plant breeders. Robert and Sarah's son, William Ormston Backhouse (1885–1962), worked with wheat in Argentina, having been trained in the new applied science of plant breeding by two of the great pioneers in the field: William Bateson and Rowland Biffen. The varieties he produced revolutionized wheat production in Argentina, but in his later years he continued in the family tradition to work on daffodils, concentrating on the red, orange, and pink tones, which his parents had done so much to pioneer.

All in all, it is estimated that some 430 varieties of daffodil were raised by the family.

The profits of prophecy

PETER BARR

PETER BARR (1826–1909) appears to have been a colourful character. Photographs show him with a full beard and wisps of hair escaping from below a beret-type hat. Descriptions of him in later life talk of him always wearing country tweeds and Scottish-style hats. The title of his book on daffodils, *Ye Narcissus or Daffodyl Flowere Containing Hys Historie and Culture*, published in 1884, indicates a kind of faux-historical style which today we would read as affectation. The book in fact doubled as a catalogue (the distinction between the two has always been ambiguous in the garden world); it and another publication put out in the same year by William Baylor Hartland, an Irish grower, were the first daffodil catalogues.

Born in Lanarkshire, Scotland, Barr started out working in a seed shop in Glasgow. Rising through the business he ended up in a partnership in Covent Garden, the market area of London which at the time completely dominated the capital's fruit, vegetable, and ornamental plant trade. From 1860 onwards he increasingly turned from seed to plants, importing plants and bulbs from the Netherlands and sourcing rarities from amateur growers and botanists. A key moment appears to have been reading *Paradisi in sole paradisus terrestris* (1629) by John Parkinson, who reported that there were ninety-four varieties of daffodil grown in Britain at the time. Very few of these were still available, a fact which appears to have led Barr to become a daffodil-obsessive. He began to collect as many old varieties as he could, as well as new ones. It was this desire to acquire as much as he could of what today we would call genetic material, that led him to organise the group which bought Edward Leeds's bulb collection. In addition he bought up bulbs from William Backhouse and Norfolk clergyman and amateur breeder George Gudgeon Nelson (1818–1882).

With a vast range of botanical booty having poured in to Britain over the last hundred years, gardeners and growers in the final decades of the nineteenth century began to join forces with botanists to try to make sense of what was rapidly becoming a confusing scene. Hybridising was now increasingly understood, accepted, and carried out, adding to the confusion of names and the complexity of classification. Barr took the initiative and worked with a Kew botanist to establish a classification system for daffodils. To launch this and to popularize the flower, he persuaded the RHS to hold a daffodil conference in the spring of 1884. One of the resolutions of the conference resulted in the formation of a Narcissus Committee, under the auspices of the society's Scientific Committee, while another drew a clear red line between horticulture and botany in declaring that a unified system of daffodil naming and classification should be based on criteria used by growers, not those by botanists. It was around this time also that the first book on daffodils since Herbert's *Amaryllidaceae* of 1837 was published—F. W. Burbidge's *The Narcissus: Its History and Culture* (1875). One irony of this first daffodil conference was that the new committee voted to abolish the latinate names of Barr's proposed categories and replace them with readily understood English ones. History does not record Barr's reaction, but he comes across as a phlegmatic man, more than able to overcome minor upsets.

During the latter part of his career, Barr became what we would now call a plant hunter, travelling to those parts of Europe where wild daffodils were numerous and varied, primarily in central and southern France, Spain, and Portugal. He came back not only with many new introductions to stimulate further breeding but was also inspired by the sight of daffodils en masse in woods and fields. He started to promote the idea of mass plantings—what we now call "naturalising"; this must have been good for business, too. His use of daffodils in this way was part of a wider movement across Europe to use plants in a more naturalistic way, the blending of garden and wild plants celebrated in William Robinson's *The Wild Garden* (1870).

In 1895 Barr took his sons into partnership, retiring from the business the next year. A year later he was one of the first recipients of the RHS Victoria Medal—the society's highest honor. Soon he was on his travels again, a total of seven years travelling around the world promoting daffodils, of which two years were spent in southern Africa. We cannot help but wonder how many daffodils the "Daffodil King," as he was known by this time, actually saw on this great expedition.

One further aspect of Barr's later work needs to be mentioned—his importation of wild daffodil bulbs from France, Spain, and Portugal. Digging up wild bulbs and exporting them has been widely practiced from the nineteenth century onwards and is only really just coming to an end—under pressure from conservationists who point out just how bad this often is for wild populations. Barr is known to have imported very large quantities of some species, to the extent that he may have had a severe long-term impact on certain species in some localities. *Narcissus triandrus* is known to have been a particular target of his company's collecting—it was sold as 'Queen of Spain'.

Barr's achievement was to bring daffodils into the gardening mainstream, but it was also to bring together the separate achievements of his predecessors. When he bought the collections of Backhouse, Leeds, and others, he was accumulating the results of separate and independent breeding work; now the fruit of their efforts would be one big genepool, and one which was being promoted with flair. How much he actually bred is open to question; of the 106 varieties registered in the name of Barr & Sons, by the time of his death in 1909, many are almost certainly selections from wild stocks or old varieties.

An eruption of diversity

GEORGE ENGLEHEART AND THE BIRTH OF THE MODERN DAFFODIL

THE LATE NINETEENTH and early twentieth century saw the broad outlines of the modern daffodil evolve, through a kind of artificial Darwinian process. Varieties survived which breeders liked—so the breeder took the place of the forces of natural selection in the evolutionary process. Different breeders bred for different features, and in these early days, these were largely aesthetic. Only later did more functional requirements such as strength of stem or plant robustness become important. An odd feature of these years is that some varieties became renowned not for what they were, but for what they could offer; the potential of their genes, in other words, was more important than the plant itself. One such was Rev. George Engleheart's 'Will Scarlett' (pre-1898) a Large-cupped variety with twisted perianth segments and a dramatic orange cup—a feature illustrating its Poeticus background. It was quite unlike anything that had yet been seen, with many disadvantages, but it was widely used for breeding by others.

Engleheart (1851–1936), who worked on daffodils between 1882 and 1923, is often spoken of as the man who really launched the modern daffodil. Like many of the Church of England's country clergy, he was interested in many things. In his case, archaeology was perhaps as much a passion as daffodil breeding: in 1924 he became involved in a dispute concerning Stonehenge between druid revivalists and archaeologists, over whether the former should be allowed to bury the ashes of their dead members there. Engleheart and fellow archaeologists were much opposed and eventually won their case. Disputes over the use of this key Stone Age monument continue to this day.

Engleheart initially worked with Leeds and Backhouse hybrids and wild species (trying to replicate some of the natural hybrids which Herbert had worked on), but he went on to do much original and

Engleheart's 'Firebrand' (Small-cupped, pre-1897) **1** is typical of many late nineteenth-century daffodils, with its star-like appearance, the perianth segments widely separated. Among his other yellows are 'Helios' (Large-cupped, pre-1912) **2** and the surprisingly modern-looking 'Mars' (Small-cupped, pre-1903) **3**. 'Will Scarlett' (Large-cupped, pre-1898) **4** was regarded by many as a breakthrough; wrote E. A. Bowles of it in the early 1930s, "Bunches of its gaudy flowers have been selling in the London shops [and] ordinary visitors to the garden always pick it out as the variety they would like to gather and carry away with them." Engleheart excelled with well-displayed white perianth segments: 'Beersheba' (Trumpet, pre-1923) **5**, 'White Emperor' (Trumpet, pre-1913) **6**, 'Mitylene' (Large-cupped, pre-1923) **7**, 'Resolute' (Large-cupped, pre-1897) **8**, and 'Evangeline' (Small-cupped, 1908) **9**. His work with Poeticus is apparent with 'White Lady' (Small-cupped, pre-1897) **10**, 'Horace' (Poeticus, pre-1894) **11**, and 'Albatross' (Small-cupped, pre-1891) **12**. A revival of interest in heirloom varieties can be appreciated with this row of Engleheart's 'Lucifer' (Small-cupped, pre-1897) **13** at New Generation Daffodils in Cornwall; the flowers of such plants are not strong and compared to modern varieties, do not stand rough weather or transport, but their relaxed floppy appearance appeals to many. ▶

adventurous breeding. He was one of the first to work with forms of Poeticus, with results which perhaps laid down tracks that have been followed ever since, as the Poeticus species introduced intense cup colours, which became typical of the Small-cupped division. Some of his varieties were particularly popular with florists in the first half of the twentieth century. He did not keep exact records, confessing as much in a letter to The Brodie (more of him in the next section) in 1917, a letter in which he also states, "I am almost stone-broke over my small bulb-farm," then in its third season. Eelworm became a problem, and in 1923 he sold his stock, devoting the remainder of his life to archaeology.

Engleheart was very productive, with over 720 cultivars to his name. Kate Donald (a former Daffodil Registrar for the RHS who, with her husband, Duncan, runs Croft 16, an heirloom daffodil collection) reckons they have more

Englehearts than anyone else. "He got carried away with the excitement of breeding, he had no plan and was not good at selecting good parents." She adds, however, that "some were very good," admitting of the palely ethereal Large-cupped 'Tenedos' and white Trumpet 'Beersheba' (both pre-1923), "If I had bred them, I would die happy." Engleheart sold both varieties to The Brodie, who we must suspect earned the benefit of them. Another popular Engleheart white was 'White Lady' (Small-cupped, pre-1897), although the Donalds point out that it appears to be a strain rather than a clone, as it shows so much variation. 'White Lady' became rapidly outdated—E. A. Bowles, the great twentieth-century writer on bulbs, described how to some its cup "suggests the remains of a slug's hearty meal," adding his own damning comment, "Do not look her in the face."

A military eye
THE BRODIE OF BRODIE

MAJOR IAN BRODIE (1868–1943)—or, to give him his full aristocratic title, The Brodie of Brodie—was a Scottish clan Laird (i.e., tribal chieftain) and professional soldier whose work on daffodils in the earlier years of the twentieth century is not remembered through any particular commercially available cultivars but through a genetic heritage and a personal legend.

The Brodie (as he was always known) had the perfect bio for a British gentleman—Eton and the Guards (i.e., the country's leading private school followed by the most elite army regiment). He was possibly inspired to take up breeding by the 1884 RHS Daffodil Conference. Almost immediately thereafter, however, he went off to fight in the Boer War. Although his family had no family links to horticulture and Brodie Castle was in a remote location, he seemed to be able to get hold of very good varieties to work with as soon as they were available, e.g., 'Apricot' and 'Victoria' (both pre-1897 Trumpets), and he had Engleheart's 'Blood Orange' (Small-cupped, pre-1904) even before it was registered. He again saw battle during World War I but devolved much to his wife, Violet, who was always a very active deputy while his staff, led by his head gardener, J. M. Annand, were involved in making crosses back home.

Whereas many other aristocratic daffodil people went off gallivanting around the country during the flowering season (probably using the opportunity to look at each other's collections as an excuse for socializing), The Brodie stayed at home with his plants. Every flower was de-anthered as it flowered (removing pollen to minimise self-fertilisation), and crosses were made and then recorded in a meticulous stud book. Between 1899 and 1942, he raised thousands of seedlings from his crosses, with trial plots organised with military precision in the old walled kitchen garden. Building very largely on varieties obtained from Engleheart (he went on to buy Engleheart's stock on his death in 1936), the Brodie made over 12,500 individual crosses but only judged 185 as being worthy of a name (although another 229 were named by those who bought stock from him). Contemporary visitors remarked on how the rows of seedlings were like soldiers on parade, three inches between them in rows eight inches apart; anything not up to scratch was ruthlessly removed to the compost heap.

The Brodie's stud books enabled the ancestry of all his seedlings to be known, and remarkably they were made accessible to anyone who wanted to see them. The books contain an amazing amount of detail, even being updated with

information on the progress of the cross, such as the amount of seed collected, the germination percentages, and finally many years later, details of the flower.

One plant which was often incorrectly attributed to him was 'Fortune'. The variety had been depleted by various misfortunes, including eelworm—from which Brodie Castle's remote location may have protected it. The Brodie ended up with the largest number of survivors and had almost a monopoly on its production. So great was the demand that he was selling them at £14 a bulb (the 1920 equivalent of £340), a good return on an original investment of four bulbs (or one—depending upon which source you believe).

The story of 'Fortune' illustrates two key points about plant breeding. The first is that it can be difficult to know who is responsible for new varieties; the second is that a variety may be valued not for its own worth, but for its genes, i.e., its potential. 'Fortune' was a Large-cupped variety, registered in 1917 by Walter T. Ware of Bath, in southwest England. The company had begun trading in 1883 and from the outset was famous for tulips and daffodils, for its trade with Dutch producers, and for its export business. It is even said that Monet got bulbs for his garden at Giverny from them. When first shown, 'Fortune' sparked a sensation: the cup was the richest orange anyone had yet seen, and the perianth segments were broad, flat, and smooth. The whole flower had a proportion and a perfection that had never before been seen. Not only was it sought after as a show plant, but breeders saw the potential to combine the striking cup and form of the plant with other characteristics, and so make their own mark on the world. When first made available, the price for one bulb was £50.

Ware produced eight other varieties of no particular note. It so happened that he had been an agent for one of the garden world's most intriguing characters of the time, Ellen Willmott (1858–1934).

Unfortunately, modern varieties were planted out at Brodie Castle in the 1980s to help liven up the garden as a visitor attraction—with grave consequence for those who want to track down original Brodie plants. The collection of Brodie varieties is in the old walled garden.

Identifying plants sometimes has to proceed through a process of elimination, this one is "not Mr Jinks" . A selection of the varieties that have been identified, largely through the work of Kate and Duncan Donald: 'Seraglio' (Small-cupped, pre-1926) **2** and, derived from it, 'Dunkeld' (Large-cupped, pre-1934) **3**; 'Nevis' (Trumpet, pre-1915) **4**, one of whose parents was the well-known 'King Alfred'; 'Coverack Perfection' (Large-cupped, pre-1930) **5**, one of the few commercially available Brodie varieties; 'Therapia' (Small-cupped, pre-1922) **6**; 'Loch Maree' (Large-cupped, pre-1940) **7**; 'Smyrna' (Poeticus, pre-1926) **8**; 'Fortune's Knight' (Large-cupped, pre-1930) **9**; and 'Cotterton' (Large-cupped, pre-1936) **1 0**. ▶

3

2

4

5

6

From 1908 to 1911 Willmott had done some daffodil breeding and won some RHS prizes for her varieties; she is said to have had a collection of more than six hundred varieties and is reputed to have made her staff install trip wires around the daffodils in the fields, which would set off air guns to frighten anyone attempting to help themselves. It seems highly likely that Ware was simply taking the credit for Willmott's work. This is not to imply any sleight of hand; as daffodils can take many years between germination and flowering, it has been quite common throughout daffodil history for growers to sell seedlings to others, who then have to make the decision about whether to pick out possible winners and propagate them.

In 1942, the RHS recognised the Brodie's work by awarding him the Victoria Medal of Horticulture. He died the following year; an obituary noted that The Brodie had for daffodils a "love and enthusiasm . . . and a delightful schoolboy quality." Many of his seedlings went to Northern Ireland, where they helped Guy Wilson and Lionel Richardson establish the province as a major centre for daffodil breeding. Only a very few are in commerce now, and only as bulbs from specialist suppliers.

When the National Trust for Scotland, a heritage conservation body, took over the estate in 1978 from the family, only a few of The Brodie's daffodils could be recognized. Searches organised by the Trust brought over a hundred of them out from under cover, from a variety of sources, including from as far away as Australia. The Brodie had had a habit of naming varieties after other notable Scottish aristocratic houses, but comparatively few of his daffodils have turned up in their gardens—one had to be very keen on daffodils to plant bulbs named after one's property, it seems. A former gardener, Leslie Forbes, in his mid-eighties, was able to label 156 varieties, and so by the early 1980s, a good collection had been assembled. Then disaster struck: the area where the daffodils were planted had not been mapped, so that when some children who were staying in one of the holiday cottages on the estate pulled out all the labels, there was no way of knowing which label belonged to which daffodil. The cultivars gathered here, several of them considered important, were once again effectively lost.

The situation at the time of writing, however, is a relatively optimistic one. Kate and Duncan Donald of Croft 16 have begun to identify the plants. While going about their work they pointed out in a report that the heritage value of the collection had been seriously compromised by the Trust's planting of modern varieties to beautify the property for visitors. In addition they questioned the late Mr. Forbes's record-keeping and some of his identifications—memory alone is rarely an accurate source of information on bulb naming. Great progress has been made, though, and a short-list of "wanted" missing varieties produced, with the hope that these can still be found in other Scottish gardens or overseas.

Another daffodil dynasty

THE WILLIAMSES OF CORNWALL

THE WILLIAMS FAMILY of Cornwall were originally from Wales but made a fortune in mining in this mineral-rich area. Like many other wealthy Cornish families they became deeply involved in gardening in the late nineteenth century, supporting the work of plant hunters, especially in the foothills of the Himalaya, in introducing a wide range of new species to horticulture. Although their gardens are now dominated by the towering magnolias, rhododendrons, and camellias so typical of this period, they also made a major contribution to daffodils. John Charles Williams (1861–1939), famous for *Camellia ×williamsii*, also bred daffodils and inspired a cousin, Percival D. Williams (1865–1935), to try his hand. P. D. Williams went on to become one of the greatest of all breeders, with four decades of productivity, beginning in 1895. His reputation is that of having an intuitive, almost mystical approach to breeding. He kept no records, or if he did, he kept them secret (his cousin claimed to have lost his camellia breeding records when his case was stolen on a night train to London, but there was always the suspicion that he never kept

any for either, and the story of the theft was simply a cover). His great achievement was the Large-cupped 'Carlton' (pre-1927), the most widely sold daffodil of all time. This became renowned as a superb garden variety and an important cut flower for an industry that became increasingly important in Cornwall from the early twentieth century onwards; it is very disease-resistant, so it is still important. P. D. Williams was fond of naming his varieties after Cornish villages; common elements include Tre- (village), Pol- (pool), Pen- (hill or headland), and the names of ancient Celtic saints. Great ones from the approximately five hundred he named (and which are still commercially important) are 'Beryl' (Cyclamineus, pre-1907), 'Trevithian' (Jonquil, pre-1927), and 'Cragford' (Tazetta, pre-1930).

Williams became very friendly with Dutchman Matthew Zandbergen (1903–1990) after visiting his collection in the Netherlands. He asked him to be his Dutch agent, and the result was that many Williams varieties went on to become mainstays of the Dutch bulb industry. The Dutch liked his varieties because Williams was one of the first breeders who thought beyond simply the look of the flower and paid great attention to a good overall habit and strong stems—characteristics the hard-headed Dutch had already decided were crucial. As an example of this, Williams is reputed to have rejected Engleheart's 'Will Scarlett' even though other breeders were using it in their crosses as much as possible; he apparently hated its narrow twisted perianths and saw no future in the plant. Apparently, he recommended that a daffodil should be judged by looking at the back first, as at the dinner table people would look at a table decoration from all sides.

Zandbergen was born on the daffodil farm of the de Graaff brothers, who were major breeders and growers of daffodils and other bulbs, where his father was manager. He would visit P. D. Williams three or four times a year and is known to have fallen for rugged Cornwall, so different to his own flat homeland. He is remembered as a first-class judge of daffodils and an effective international ambassador for the plant, warmly hosting growers from other countries at home, taking them to Dutch shows, and, being an inveterate traveller himself, always on the lookout for new varieties which growers back home could make use of. He bought plants from many breeders, but not all were forthcoming. In 1939 he visited Guy Wilson in Northern Ireland and offered him £100 for a good seedling. Getting "no" for an answer, he upped the price several more times but never shifted the canny Irish grower.

P. D. Williams's son Michael (1903–1963) kept up the daffodil business and the links with Zandbergen. He bred 'St. Keverne', a classic yellow Large-cupped (pre-1934) that had good resistance to the basal rot fungus which killed many others in wet Cornwall, as well as good resistance to the ever-present Cornish wind. However as it was planted in increasing quantities it fell victim to virus instead and so is now much less important commercially. It was outlived on the bulb farms by his father's 'Carlton', which is largely virus-resistant and still important for the cut-flower trade.

J. C. Williams's 'Hospodar' (Large-cupped, pre-1914) **1**. An article in the American Horticultural Society's 1937 issue of *The American Daffodil Year Book* hailed P. D. Williams's 'Killigrew' (Large-cupped, pre-1907) **2** as "another of [his] most beautiful flowers. Perfect in form, balance, and quality [with] exceptional vigor and rapid increase." Also by P. D. is 'Brunswick' (Large-cupped, pre-1931) **3**. His 'Larkelly' **4** is

a dwarf Cyclamineus (pre-1930)—the Williams family were among early experimenters with Cyclamineus, although few crosses were named; also in this division: the very early 'Peeping Tom' (pre-1948) **5** and 'Beryl' **6**. 'Carlton' AGM **7** was his great success. 'Coverack Glory' (pre-1927) **8** was another fine Large-cupped variety. Michael Williams's 'Jack Snipe' (pre-1951) **9** is among the most successful Cyclamineus of all time.

Thinking small

ALEC GRAY MINIATURES

FROM P. D.'S ERA on, daffodil breeding diversified, with many more people becoming entranced, obsessed, and determined to breed new colours, new combinations of colours, better plants, and novel shapes. At the same time, though, it consolidated, largely concerned with perfecting the "standard" daffodil, be it Trumpet, Large-, or Small-cupped. One man stands out from the next generation, for his prescience in choosing a novel direction which is finally coming into its own.

Alec Gray (1895–1986), like Engleheart, was an amateur archaeologist, as well as a fruit grower and raiser of 110 new daffodils over fifty-nine years of active breeding. Working as a farm manager on the Scillies in the 1920s,

he established a collection of daffodils, beginning to register varieties from the late 1930s onwards. Gray's triumph was the immensely successful 'Tête-à-Tête', which he produced sometime in the 1940s. By 2006 it made up thirty-four percent of Dutch bulb production, being grown on 560ha (1,400 acres) of the country, with seventeen million pots sold at auction. From the same cross, Gray raised two other very good varieties, 'Jumblie' and 'Quince'. 'Tête-à-Tête' was the first real success of a new kind of daffodil, not just a robust and charming miniature but a complex cross between divisions. It and its siblings were descended from one unknown parent and 'Cyclataz', a 1920s cross made by Arthur Tait, in Portugal; 'Tête-à-Tête'

is actually a pun on Tait's name rather than a reference to there being two flowers atop one stem. 'Cyclataz' is in turn a cross between 'Soleil d'Or', an old (pre-1731) Tazetta, and the strange diminutive little *Narcissus cyclamineus*.

It was no coincidence that Gray got 'Cyclataz' in Portugal, as he and his wife, Flomay, would often go travelling in Spain and Portugal to collect more-small natural forms. He went on to produce many other great and innovative miniatures, although some of these do not perform well in cool summer climates—to name but two, the beautiful, pale little Tazetta 'Minnow' (1962) and the almost perfectly round 'Sun Disc', a pre-1946 Jonquil.

Concluding our brief survey of these crucial years in the making of the modern daffodil, it is worth remembering that there is almost no mention of genetic science in the form of Mendelian principles in any of the writings about these early breeders. Mendel's work was effectively discovered in 1900, and introduced to science through a series of conferences on hybridisation, in London, Paris, and New York, over the next few years. It took a long time for Mendelian genetics to be understood and used effectively, however, with the breeders of ornamental plants among the last to be "converted" to the new way of thinking. It would probably be true to say that not until after World War II did breeders pay it much attention.

A selection of Alec Gray miniatures. 'Tête-à-Tête' AGM **1** is well on its way to evicting 'King Alfred' and 'Carlton' from the "most popular daffodil of all time" slot. 'Elka' (Trumpet, 1989) **2**, also very early, deserves a great future. 'Jumblie' (Miscellaneous, pre-1952) **3**, from the same cross as 'Tête-à-Tête', is popular as a rock garden or container plant. 'Johanna' is a dwarf Triandrus (pre-1950) **4**. A display by Broadleigh Gardens of Somerset illustrates Alec Gray's work; they hold the UK National Collection of his daffodils **5**.

Travelling, Changing, and Multiplying

THE NINETEENTH CENTURY

The nineteenth century saw the British fan out all over the world, and while they may have, for a period, governed vast stretches, they actually tended to settle only in those climates which had some resemblance to what they knew at home. With them went their language, culture, crops, and garden plants. Daffodils and Britishers took root in similar climes, and today it should come as no surprise that the United States, New Zealand, and Australia are home to growers and enthusiasts.

Ireland, Britain's first colony, has a mild and moist climate ideal for daffodils. Nurseryman William Baylor Hartland (1836–1912) even tried to get the daffodil to be made the country's national flower but failed in the face of the humble shamrock. Hartland's grandfather had come to Ireland from London's Kew Gardens to set up a nursery, which Hartland eventually inherited. While he grew a variety of crops, it was daffodils which clearly inspired Hartland the most. In an early version of the heirloom plant rescue, and a parallel with Peter Barr, starting around 1880, Hartland searched for old varieties all over Ireland, digging up as many different bulbs from gardens as he could, to then bulk them up in the nursery and offer them for sale. His first catalogue, *A Little Book of Daffodils: Nearly 100 Varieties as Offered and Collected by W. B.*

Hartland (1884), mined the same vein of pseudo-historical whimsy which Barr had exploited, but taken to even further lengths and using an antique typeface.

The following random example of Hartland's prose gives a good idea of his style:

> Oh! Amadis! Never saw I so sweet a maid in all my life before, nor likewise one with eyes so bright, and countenance so gentle and yet, withal, so arch. I saw that her arms were all overladen with Daffodillies, like a great cluster of beauteous stars. And so she walked amid the flowers that reached nigh to her knees and came, and was gone, leaving me lying as though entranced with what I had beholden.

Hartland's catalogue helped inspire Ireland's first major breeder, Guy Wilson

(1885–1962), who was apparently first shown it as a child by his mother, when he asked her if white daffodils existed. He started growing daffodils in his teens and, being sent away to boarding school, had to rely on his mother's letters for information on their flowering and performance. Starting to breed daffodils in his early twenties, he went on to dedicate his life to them, dubbing the love of the flower as the "yellow fever." He was known to work on his plants by moonlight, or if this was inadequate, by torchlight. White flowers remained a lifelong obsession, although he also worked with many other colours. He is known to have visited The Brodie many times. The area where he was brought up, around Ballymena in County Antrim (in the British-governed north), has remained a centre of daffodil breeding ever since, with many of the very best and most prolific breeders originating here.

New Zealand became one of the most accommodating homes away from home for the British. The tradition of the flower and produce show, which became firmly established in villages across Britain in the nineteenth century, was soon transplanted to these islands on the other side of the world. As early as 1898, the Wellington Horticultural Society started a show dedicated entirely to daffodils, and a thriving nursery and daffodil breeding business soon got going. As often happens in pioneering societies, homesteads were built and abandoned with speed, and nowadays clumps of

Some Irish-bred daffodils. 'Cantatrice' (pre-1936) **1**, a Guy Wilson Trumpet, illustrates this great Irish breeder's passion to create the perfect white daffodil. The daffodil cognoscenti rate Lionel Richardson as the next greatest Irish breeder; he was certainly prolific. Of his 640-plus registered varieties, here are three, all Large-cupped: 'Pinza' (1962) **2**, 'Rainbow' (1961) **3**, and 'Vulcan' (1956) **4**.

1

Double 'Kiwi Magic' (Max Hamilton, 1989) **1** and Small-cupped 'Little Jewel' **2** (Jim O'More, pre-1985) were both bred in New Zealand. 'Binkie' (Large-cupped, pre-1938) **3** is one of the best-established reverse bicolours, fading to a uniform pale yellow; grown and selected by the Australian W. Wolfhagen from seed supplied by Irishman Guy Wilson, it illustrates the global collaboration which has long been a feature of the daffodil world.

daffodils are often the only sign of a place where a settler's home once stood.

Australia too saw daffodil growing take off, but only to any extent in the southern colonies of Tasmania and Victoria, the rest of the continent being too hot and dry. A writer in the 1938 *Daffodil Yearbook* noted of Tasmania that "it is difficult to get a bunch of good daffodils intact to their destination through the streets of Hobart, for many people will stop to admire and talk about them with real love and admiration." Despite strict quarantine restrictions limiting the importation of bulbs and so limiting the ability of breeders to innovate, daffodil growing and breeding continues.

It was in the United States that daffodils really took off. A trickle of bulbs in the early 1800s had become a flood of Dutch imports by the end of the century.

Before we turn to U.S. soil, it is worth a brief look at the source of these imports. The Netherlands is the only non-English-speaking country to fall in love with the daffodil, but it has happened in a very different way. The Dutch are well known for their love of the tulip, which led to the extraordinary story of the world's first financial bubble, the "tulip mania" of the seventeenth century. It was almost inevitable that Dutch growers would turn to daffodil production during the nineteenth century, as growers began to look to building an export trade in plants. Trade is very much what Dutch daffodil growing is about—there is no equivalent of the keen amateur interest in growing and exhibiting or breeding daffodils that typifies anglophone countries; growing daffodil is business. In this sense the daffodil is not a cult flower in the

Netherlands as it does not have an amateur enthusiast following.

The Dutch attitude to plant production has always tended to be very focussed on profitability. One consequnece of this is that government support for growers in the form of research into propagation, cultivation, and disease management has tended to be high. W. F. Leenen & Sons are regarded as the number one breeders and growers in the Netherlands. Established in 1954, the company invested in building up a collection to use as a gene bank (now consisting of nearly two thousand cultivars) and developing international links: they have trial grounds in Britain, Chile, Brazil, and Australia. As well, they have done pioneering work in establishing chipping bulbs as a propagation technique.

Some growers have tended to look at the Dutch rather suspiciously, one California-based breeder for example, Harold Koopowitz, saying, "The Dutch are always on the lookout for new material—a lot of breeders are a bit wary of them. They take a variety and then get it mass produced, leaving the breeder out of the loop."

"Dutch" still carries with it an enormous cachet in the United States when it comes to bulbs, giving a definite advantage to Dutch companies. Early settlers, however, brought their daffodils with them—their ability to survive for long periods as dry bulbs must have helped their journey across the Atlantic. Consequently, small hotspots of naturalising bulbs built up soon, especially in Virginia. The later years of the nineteenth century saw immense imports from the Netherlands, but this went into sharp decline with the 1919 Plant Quarantine Act, which finally stopped importation of bulbs in 1926 for several decades. This stimulated home production, with a number of Dutch firms setting up on Long Island, in the coastal Virginia area, and in places between Portland and Seattle, such as the Skagit Valley. Jan de Graaff, a member of the leading Dutch nursery family, went to Portland in 1926 to set up bulb farms,

Two of the many daffodils bred by the de Graaffs in the Netherlands: the dwarf and early 'February Silver' (Trumpet, pre-1949) **1** and 'Garden Princess' (Large-cupped, pre-1952) **2**.

investing in breeding as well as production, but after naming around fifty varieties he sold off the daffodils in 1959 and concentrated on lilies, for which the business became world famous. The Pacific Northwest was for a while a major producer of bulbs, the high point being the 1940s, when twenty scientists and sixty-nine research projects were working on bulb production and pest and disease control.

Breeding in the United States began to develop in the interwar years, but many varieties were never registered, or bulbs were distributed privately, and very little from this period remains. One breeder who started work at this time was more businesslike: Grant E. Mitsch (1907–1989) in Oregon was the first to give his seedlings proper publicity and distribution. He produced a catalogue showing the parentage of his varieties and set up educational exhibits at shows.

Mitsch started breeding in the early 1930s, building up to an annual output of around one hundred crosses. There was a high public awareness of the potential of plant breeding at this time, thanks to the work of Luther Burbank (1849–1936), whose California nursery had produced a vast number of hybrids in a wide range of ornamental and crop plants, amidst considerable publicity. Mitsch's daughter, Elise Havens, a breeder herself, recalls her father's pioneering spirit. "He did have quite a number of Luther Burbank publications and often mentioned his admiration for his ability to look at a group of seedlings and to ascertain immediately which ones would likely be successful." Altogether Mitsch registered around seven hundred varieties; Elise recalls her father's process:

> [He would make] crosses involving perhaps twenty flowers, to give enough quantity to see a reasonable picture of the capability of a cultivar as a parent. He once repeated a successful cross using hundreds of flowers and came to the conclusion that was not a very practical route to success—it seemed wiser to use great care in the selection of parents to be used in one's breeding programme. He did a lot of work in the upper divisions [i.e., divisions 5 to 9], which were not nearly as popular then as they are now[,] emphasized deep colour, and attempted to produce true red cup colour from the pink end, instead of orange.

The first known daffodil show in the United States was run by the Maryland Daffodil Society in 1924, with the Garden Club of Virginia setting up shows ten years later. This latter group had already played a major role in promoting the flower; the club's president, Leslie H. Gray, set up a system of daffodil test gardens in different parts of the state in 1930. Fifty varieties were chosen to represent the system of classification and to illustrate to members and the public the range and performance of daffodils. Local clubs which belonged to or were affiliated with the garden club were encouraged to set up daffodil committees and carry out their own testing programmes. Led by the Virginians, interest in daffodils grew, and in 1955 the American Daffodil Society was formed.

A selection of Grant Mitsch's prodigious output of daffodils: 'Small Talk' (Trumpet, 1965) **1**, 'Precocious' AGM (Large-cupped, 1976) **2**, 'Plover' (Large-cupped, 1975) **3**, 'Lemon Brook' (Large-cupped, 1991) **4**, and 'Butterscotch' (Large-cupped, 1962) **5**. His work among the upper divisions produced many good Cyclamineus, appreciated by gardeners worldwide for reliable early colour: 'Surfside' AGM (1972) **6**, 'Itzim' AGM (1982) **7**, 'Lemon Silk' (1987) **8**, and 'Frostkist' (1968) **9**. 'Oryx' AGM (1979) **1 0** is a Jonquil, while like many breeders he produced a modest number of Split-coronas, such as 'Trigonometry' AGM (1995) **1 1**. ▶

Establishing order

THE WORLD OF DAFFODIL GROWERS

IN THE INTRODUCTION I referred to the daffodil as a cult plant. One of the distinguishing marks of a cult plant is a structure: societies, shows, competitions, rules for judging plant quality and performance, and an agreed system for classifying and naming plant varieties. Such an "organisational infrastructure" is well established for daffodils, although we can be certain that ninety-nine percent of the people who grow daffodils in their gardens are unaware of it.

Central to the daffodil world is the registration of variety names. In the past, varieties would be regularly renamed when they crossed borders or another nurseryman started growing them. Registration fixes a name and the claim of a particular individual (or more rarely, a company) to have originated it. The Royal Horticultural Society started its register in 1884, with a paid post of registrar being officially created in 1923. The current registrar is Sharon McDonald, who came to the job after working at the herbarium at the Royal Botanic Gardens at Kew. "Registration," she says, "is based on a description of the flower and other aspects of the plant provided by the breeder—parentage is not so important, in fact it is not always known." Nor is registration like patenting; as Sharon explains, "It is not my job to pronounce something as being different or

unique—it is up to the raiser of the daffodil to ensure uniqueness." Patenting, in the form of application for Plant Breeders' Rights, is rarely applied for ("only on about two to five plants a year, mostly from Dutch breeders," she says). New registrations come in at around two to three hundred a year, mostly from the traditional anglophone breeding countries, or the Netherlands, but Sharon acknowledges a recent "surge" from Japan and some new arrivals, such as the Czech Republic and Latvia.

Of the twenty-seven thousand unique daffodil varieties registered, Sharon reckons that only about ten percent are available commercially. The register can be accessed from the RHS website, where basic information on the plant is provided.

Most countries with a reasonable number of growers have a daffodil society. The United Kingdom's Daffodil Society was set up in 1898 as the Midland Daffodil Society, becoming national in 1963. In April 1998 the World Daffodil Council was established to co-ordinate the activities of societies in the United States, United Kingdom, Australia, New Zealand, and the Netherlands. Societies publish newsletters, organise shows and local groups, and generally promote the plant.

Shows are a crucial part of the daffodil business, and indeed are absolutely central to the notion of a cult plant, as is the fact that the shows are competitive. They are an occasion for amateur growers to exhibit flowers which they have grown to perfection, and for breeders to introduce new varieties. Among amateurs there is often an overlap with other cult plants grown for competition, with daffodil exhibitors also showing summer flowers like sweet peas and dahlias, at least in Britain. In talking to judges it seems as if there was a time when rivalry used to be quite intense, but growers these days seem more prepared to share knowledge and a more generous spirit prevails.

The demographic description of those who grow and show has historically been that of older men from skilled working class backgrounds, although many of the breeders have tended to be highly educated or members of the gentry. Small shows happen in village halls or in facilities provided by nurseries or garden centres. National shows are grander events and have the added excitement of attracting new varieties from breeders. In Britain many shows happen as an adjunct to RHS flower shows, encouraging general gardeners to wander down the aisles of green hessian–lined staging to discover something of the world behind the flowers they will all have in their gardens but think little about outside flowering time.

The prizes for plants in daffodil shows are hardly enough to cover the cost of fuel needed to get to the event. Growers enter for recognition, and breeders in the hope of launching their creations. At a national level, achievement is recognized by a series of awards; in Britain the Ralph B. White Memorial Medal is, for example, awarded to the raiser of the best new daffodil cultivar exhibited at the RHS during the year, while the Peter Barr Memorial Cup is a kind of lifetime achievement award, presented each year by the RHS to someone who has made a significant contribution to daffodils.

The International Daffodil Register run by Britain's Royal Horticultural Society is an invaluable tool for researching the flowers. Basic data on varieties is available online; here is its paper version alongside some daffodils cut for identification at Brodie Castle.

Shows are an important part of the daffodil world. An exhibit illustrates the work of modern breeders at an RHS show **1**. Competitive exhibits of daffodils are set out in various classes, where every flower has to be arranged to conform to certain standards. Judging involves the intense deliberation of small groups of men (very few women as yet), assessing how good the flower is according to a variety of criteria, such as "poise" (its angle of presentation), whether the petals are flat, free of wrinkles, and of good substance, etc.; and awarding it points based on their assessment **2**-**6**. ▶

Midas Touch

River Queen

Carol Lombard

Moo

Fine Romance

Crackington

Dauman

Conversion

Ice

94

What the judges rate highly at shows is an important influence on what varieties are grown more widely by enthusiasts, which eventually influences what nurseries grow and the public buys. However, as so often happens in plant breeding history, "what the judges like, the public doesn't necessarily like," as contemporary breeder Harold Koopowitz points out, explaining that, for example, "judges tend to like flat and round, whereas the public like some negative space." Kate Donald, another sceptic of the judging process, points out that show rules stress "smooth, overlapping perianth segments with no gaps—so not propeller- or star-like—a deep colour, and thick substance," which makes showing old varieties or those with innovative features impossible.

The global daffodil community now has access to a unique resource, DaffSeek, which since 2006 has made available detailed information on daffodil varieties to anyone with a computer and Internet connection. While its approximately 23,000 entries do not include all the cultivars in the RHS Registry, it includes all modern ones, and information on some unregistered historic ones. DaffSeek's value and success can be seen as being part of the global citizen knowledge bank of which Wikipedia and other volunteer-created and -supported databanks are part, although those in the know do point out that information entered is usually unmoderated and therefore not always accurate. Volunteers from all over the world contribute data and regularly participate in updating it. One volunteer, Lachlan Keown from New Zealand, contributed programmes for showing the pedigrees of featured varieties and for their descendants, a feature of the site which has made DaffSeek a vital tool for anyone interested in hybridising. With a few keystrokes it is possible to bring up all the varieties registered by a particular breeder, trace the development of a particular division over time, trace back the pedigree of a variety, analyse the varieties used for breeding in a particular year, and so forth and so on. A strong feature is the inclusion of photographs, including prints of historical varieties. Needless to say, it was a valuable research tool in the writing of this book. No other group of plants is as well served.

Cornwall

CENTRE OF THE
DAFFODIL UNIVERSE

Cornwall may no longer be the centre of daffodil production either globally (the Netherlands produces more) or nationally within the United Kingdom (Lincolnshire's acreage is larger), but in terms of history and culture, the flower plays a unique role here. The Dutch and Lincolnshire industries are just that, industries, with all the hard-headed commercialism that the word implies. Daffodils there feel like just another crop.

Lincolnshire is an area of eastern England geologically similar to the Netherlands—flat and fertile, and with a long history of Dutch influence. Forcing daffodils for flower is a big part of the business there, with bulbs being chilled and then forced in glasshouses, often being destroyed afterwards. This is the only way the county can keep ahead of Cornwall, as flowering times can be four weeks later. Milder winters have eroded this advantage however, causing problems for growers. Forcing—for sale either as pot plants or for cut flowers—was also the mainstay of the Dutch daffodil industry, from the early days.

The first commercial growing in Lincolnshire started in the 1880s, with enough growers by 1903 for them to form a Daffodil Society. At around this time one grower, A. M. Wilson, recalls buying a single bulb of 'Lucifer' (Large-cupped, pre-1890) from Barr for a guinea (i.e., £1 and 1 shilling), which he later had enough stock of to sell for £100. In writing a memoir of the period in the 1939 *Daffodil Yearbook*, he recalls this as "a poor thin-petalled, short-stemmed little thing." 'Lucifer' is now a cherished heirloom variety.

At the end of a long peninsula fingering its way into the Atlantic is Cornwall, the most southwesterly part of England—though many Cornish people might object to its being referred to that way! The county has its own language, a Celtic tongue close to Welsh until it became extinct around 1914; local patriots are now reviving the language as an expression of the county's heritage. Along with its unique history, Cornwall has an unusual climate—like parts of California, it can be difficult to tell whether it is summer or winter. Moderated by the sea and the westerly winds which blow off it, its weather tends to be mild, moist, and blustery at all times of year. Wherever you are, the wind is rarely far from you. A long and complex geological history has led to its having had an important mining industry for much of its human history, but poor soils for farming. During the nineteenth century, agriculture began to focus on plantings which made the most of the county's climatic advantages, in particular the early mild springs, and minimised its geographically imposed disadvantages; these niche crops were early potatoes, cauliflowers—and daffodils.

The British daffodil crop is now around 4,000ha (10,000 acres), half the world's production, with Cornwall being about forty percent of that. Nearly all this production is based in West Cornwall and the Scilly Isles, which have the most maritime climate. Commercial growing started in the late nineteenth century, with the revolution brought about by rail transport—flowers could be picked one day and be in London markets the next. Road transport could not compete until the 1950s. In 1885, Andrew Lawry was one of many farmers who started daffodil farming in the area with the balmiest climate, on the slopes opposite St. Michael's Mount, at Varfell on the south coast. At 400ha (1,000 acres), Varfell Farm is now the world's largest daffodil producer.

Daffodil production anywhere potentially involves two outputs: bulbs for

In parts of Cornwall, anyone walking one of the many footpaths which crisscross the landscape is liable to suddenly come across a field of daffodils **1**. Now no longer used for crops, steep terraced fields in favourable south-facing locations would once have been used for wheat, potatoes, and daffodils **2**.

commercial and amateur growers and flowers for the cut-flower industry; the balance between these two will vary from place to place, depending on the variety and on local conditions. Bulbs for the cut-flower trade usually stay only two or three years in the ground. After this, their production of offsets results in crowding and a drop-off in quality, so they need to be lifted, divided, and sorted, and then the best ones replanted. Those not planted may end up being sold to the wholesale bulb trade for planting in parks and gardens or to other growers who grow them on a few more years, again for lifting and resale.

Lifting is usually done in June, the driest month (not that this means that much in Cornwall). Medium-sized bulbs are generally sold, with growers keeping the largest for cut-flower production, and the smallest to grow on. Most commercial varieties take two years to double the weight of the bulb clusters resulting from planting, so about half the stock is sold after lifting. Given the various disease problems the plants suffer from, most growers prefer to replant

their own stock. Bulbs are usually given hot-water treatment against eelworm before replanting.

Crop rotation is vital for certain crops, owing to the build-up of pests and diseases in soil if the same species is grown for many years in the same place; for daffodils the problems can be considerable and long-lasting. As a result, growers ideally like to grow on "virgin land," where daffodils have not been grown in living memory; consequently, many grow their crops on fields rented from other farmers.

Growers producing flowers for the cut-flower trade have always tried to get as long a season as possible, with four months, January to April, being generally possible. Consequently there has always been a tendency to grow a wide range of varieties to spread the season. Given that the production of flowers is always very dependent on weather—warm sun bringing them on early, a storm the next week breaking many stems—there are very high levels of contingency built in, so many more flowers are produced than can be picked.

Traditional yellow Trumpet or Large-cupped varieties may still predominate in Cornwall's bulb fields, but the range of varieties grown steadily increases and gets more adventurous every year to satisfy an increasingly sophisticated floristry market. Since the 1960s, daffodils have been picked in bud.

Picking is hard work, traditionally done by migrant workers, now mostly from eastern Europe, and often by young people who do it for a few years before settling down to other jobs.

Flower picking, like much traditional agricultural work, is poorly paid, physically demanding, and often very unpleasant, with workers starting work at dawn, often picking in driving rain or the sullen drizzle which is so much a feature of west coast climates. Picking has yet to be mechanized, so thousands of workers are needed in Cornwall during the picking season. Pay is generally piece-rate with a checker totting up each worker's totals; needless to say, each bud picked has to be perfect, with a 28cm (11-inch) stem. Wages are usually paid at the end of the day. In the past, much labour was local, or supplied by Gypsies and other itinerant travelers. Now much of the workforce are seasonal migrants from eastern Europe. Protective gloves are a must, as daffodil sap contains toxins which discourage animals from eating the otherwise lush-looking leaves, and which cause a nasty rash with prolonged exposure. Daffodil rash has always been a problem for pickers, but modern materials for gloves has now minimised the risk.

Wind is inescapable in Cornwall, and so windbreaks have long been used, particularly on the Scilly Isles. A county agricultural experimental station even made a study of the subject, ending up promoting Monterey pine (*Pinus radiata*), Leyland cypress (*Cupressus* ×*leylandii*), and, at a lower height, varieties of *Escallonia*. Growers on the Scillies have traditionally used *Pittosporum crassifolium* and *Olearia traversii*, both New Zealand shrubs very tolerant of salt-laden winds but vulnerable to long periods of freezing, and rarely grown on the mainland.

Particular individuals have played a role in the development of Cornwall's daffodil industry. Chief among them was Dan du Plessis (1924–2001), whose father was a South African soldier who came to Europe to fight in World War I and moved to Cornwall after being demobbed. Dan and his brother Peter started trading in 1953, growing daffodils for cutting but diversifying into the bulb business and breeding in the 1960s. Dan went on to win many awards, building up a large collection of high-quality varieties and inspiring many younger breeders in the process. In particular he acted as a link between growers and breeders.

In an industry where different regions can offer each other stiff competition, the ability of a particular area to keep up with the latest in technology and research is vital. Walter Abbiss (1893–1967), horticultural superintendent for Cornwall for an incredible forty years, from 1923 to 1963, was one such key figure, doing much to inform and interest growers in modern production and marketing methods and in promoting hot-water treatment against eelworm.

Matthew Zandbergen also played an important role in the Cornish daffodil business, as we heard in the last chapter, and is remembered as having had a particular love of Cornwall. He was friendly not only with the Williamses but with many other U.K. and U.S. growers, acting as something of an intermediary between them all. Despite his reputation as someone who was always on the

'Brideshead' (Large-cupped, 2002) and others bred at Rosewarne EHS, in fields at Fentongollan Farm, Cornwall.

lookout for varieties to take back home to the Netherlands, he also did much to promote traffic in the reverse direction, selling modern Dutch varieties to Cornish growers in the 1950s and so helping regenerate the industry after the war.

A significant and unusual part of the Cornish daffodil story concerns the Rosewarne Experimental Horticultural Station, which ran a daffodil breeding programme from 1963 to 1989, near Camborne on the north coast. The station was set up by the Ministry of Agriculture, Fisheries and Food to undertake research into the specific problems of farmers and growers in Cornwall. This was the golden age of government funding for agriculture and horticulture and, globally, a rare example of public funding for flower growing. Among ornamental plants, daffodils were the major priority. At the time, it was felt that private breeders were too narrowly concerned with novelty and perfection rather than what mattered to growers: disease resistance, early flowering, durability, long stems (essential for cut flowers), and good buds (as most would be sold in bud).

An early priority was early flowering; a key variety used was 'Rijnveld's Early Sensation', a short Trumpet bred originally by F. Herbert Chapman in England, of unknown parentage, sometime before 1943, but only registered in 1956 by F. Rijnveld & Sons of Holland. This was not the first time English growers might feel aggrieved at Dutch nurseries taking their plants and renaming them—a constant problem in plant breeding history. One of the resulting Rosewarne crosses, the very early Large-cupped 'Tamara' (1980), remains important today.

In 1968 Rosewarne attention was turned to Tazettas, specifically early and vigorous bold-coloured varieties; it was felt at the time that this division had too little attention from breeders. A very early New Zealand–bred variety was used, 'Autumn Sol' (1961); 'Innisidgen' (1982) was one outcome, still important and one of the first to flower on the Scillies, where Tazettas are an important crop.

Head breeder at Rosewarne was Barbara Fry, who had come originally to Cornwall as a wartime Land Girl. Like all breeders she swapped material with others and was always on the lookout for good new sources. One she found was a breeder in Maryland, Harry Tuggle; after he died in 1969 she managed to get hold of most of his stock, including many young crosses, yet to flower. These included one she named 'Hugh Town', for the capital of the Scillies, a very early Tazetta, and the now very widely grown 'Martinette' (1985); interestingly, she also produced a Tazetta named for Dan du Plessis (1996) from the same parents as 'Martinette'. One of Tuggle's greatest successes (but only via Rosewarne) was 'Cornish Chuckles' (1996), a cross between 'Matador' (one of the parents of 'Martinette' and 'Dan du Plessis') and *Narcissus cyclamineus*. 'Cornish Chuckles' is thought by many to be one of the best dwarf varieties of the last few decades— it is under 30cm (1 foot).

The Rosewarne station was closed in 1989, despite a valiant local campaign by growers and experts, the victim of Prime Minister Margaret Thatcher's privatisation of much publicly owned property. Some five hundred clones are throught to have passed into the industry from Rosewarne, and many would argue that the potential of their seedlings was still being realized in the late 2000s.

Daffodil fields beyond the sea

IN 1870, SCILLY ISLES farmer William Trevellick packed some daffodils into an old hatbox and posted it off to the great flower, fruit, and vegetable market of Covent Garden. Two weeks later he was delighted to get a cheque for "seven and six," i.e., seven shillings and six pence (now 35p, but worth £28). More boxes followed, and then with demand proving high, he offered neighbours the chance to join him. Before long, the Lord Proprietor of the Scillies and landlord of much of the islands, Thomas Algernon Dorrien-Smith, observed what was happening, and being a relatively progressive and business-minded member of his class (which many British aristocrats were spectacularly not) saw the potential and spent around £10,000 (£0.75 million today) on a trip to Holland to buy bulbs. He also encouraged the planting of hedges as shelter against the ever-present westerly winds. Dorrien-Smith was keen to develop the economy of the islands, as when he took over as Lord Proprietor, there was much desperate poverty, with kelp-burning (for fertiliser) being one of the few industries, many islanders depending on welfare handouts of food, and smuggling not unknown.

By 1885, around sixty tonnes of daffodils were being dispatched annually, rising to 635 tonnes in 1905. The islands had acquired a whole new industry. As time went on, and mainland Cornwall also began to produce more and more early daffodils, the Scilly Island farmers increasingly had to specialize. What worked for them were the Mediterranean-origin Tazettas, which make the most of the Scilly environment—mild, but drier than Cornwall and with sandy soils; these began to flower in early January.

Early growers planted their daffodil crops in very small fields as near to the sea as possible to get the greatest advantage of the ocean's warming influence; proving uneconomic during the latter part of the twentieth century, most have been abandoned to rough grass, gorse, and bracken, but among which daffodil flowers often valiantly struggle.

During the course of the twentieth century it was discovered that burning straw on the ground above Tazetta bulbs helped to improve growth; during the 1970s research showed that ethylene in the smoke stimulated early flowering—but only for Tazettas; this gas plays a part in regulating a wide range of plant processes, especially the maturing of flowers and fruit. The islands produced little straw and shipping it in was expensive, but growers found that covering the ground with plastic sheeting and pumping in smoke used the straw more efficiently.

'Scilly White', the daffodil which launched the Scilly Isles flower industry, an old dwarf Tazetta of unknown origin dating back to the 1860s and possibly older.

Growing the earliest daffodils in England

THE TAMAR VALLEY GROWERS

THE TAMAR VALLEY is a long, branching fjord of an estuary whose tidal branches penetrate deep into Cornwall, its main course acting as the boundary between Devon and Cornwall. Some of its valley sides are extremely steep and are now covered in scrub and young woodland; every now and again, anyone who explores the often dense undergrowth may come across a ruined shed, a wall, or some other sign that this area was once cultivated and used.

Indeed, these slopes were once very intensively cultivated, with workers tending fruit, flowers, and vegetables in plots which they called gardens. All produce, materials, and tools had to be laboriously carried up or down. Workers might be quite close to each other but separated by a long plunge down, followed by an equally long haul back up, so they shouted and sung to each other from one incline to another. The area was so densely cultivated that it was said that even the railway lines were edged with

Unusual daffodil varieties for sale in buckets by the side of the road in the Tamar Valley.

rhubarb. Now, all this has life and activity has almost entirely vanished.

The reason for the intense cultivation of the Tamar Valley, which really lasted less than a hundred years, was its combination of warm south- and west-facing slopes and the water, which moderates temperatures. Frosts were rare and light, and spring came early, almost earlier than anywhere else in Britain. This climate had been exploited for fruit growing since the 1700s, but in the late nineteenth century, local growers began to try other crops. Several local mines had recently shut down, so there was plenty of hardworking labor available to turn its hands and minds to new economic activity. Disease was making tree fruit uneconomic—another driver of change. Finally, starting in 1849, the railways had arrived, making it possible to grow short-lived, high-value crops and sell them to distant cities.

Strawberries came first, then daffodils, and finally a great many other flower and florist crops, such as anemones and irises, along with rhubarb and other speciality crops. Daffodils really got going in the early years of the twentieth century with 'Van Sion' (now called 'Telamonius Plenus'), a messy double dating back to the seventeenth century; 'Maximus', a Trumpet variety with an even longer history; 'Ornatus', a Poeticus type of recent French origin; and 'Golden Spur', a Trumpet discovered in a Dutch garden in the 1880s.

What really launched the daffodil trade, however, was the discovery, allegedly by a local farmer, Septimus Jackson,

A pub sign in the Tamar Valley celebrates the area's daffodil-growing heritage. The artist is Rob Rowland.

Daffodils long ago discarded onto the steep banks around fields known as "Cornish hedges" have often survived and flourished over many decades—they are a rich source of heirloom varieties.

This old flower packing shed in the Tamar Valley was found by photographer Jo Whitworth while photographing daffodils for this book. As well as the old labels and the kettle, there were "even old work coats still hanging on nails on the wall—it was incredibly atmospheric."

of a new variety in a hedge, sometime in the 1880s. A double Poeticus type, white and with a heavy scent, the late-flowering plant was quickly dubbed 'Tamar Double White'. By modern standards it is not a particularly attractive flower, but the scent was clearly something special. It also had a reputation for being difficult outside the valley. It took until the 1920s for there to be enough of it to become a worthwhile crop, but then it really took off and became a mainstay for the valley's growers. Perhaps what made it really popular was its popularity as church decoration for the Whitsun festival, on the cusp of spring and summer. After World War II, however, disease problems caused it to go into decline; it is rarely seen today.

The heyday of the Tamar Valley was probably the 1950s, when up to ten thousand people could be working here at the height of the spring season, which is more than the entire population today. Each "garden" was almost invariably a family-run affair, but during the spring and other busy times, migrant labor and more importantly part-timers joined in; many of the latter were men who worked elsewhere during the day but wanted to earn extra money in the evenings.

Managing such steep slopes was a problem, and delayed mechanization until the late 1950s. Local ingenuity often came to the fore; for example, the invention of the "earth-car," which was an old car, stripped down and with a wooden axle attached to the driveshaft, used to power a winch to pull either a plough or a container. When used for plowing, the wife usually drove the engine while

Another "Cornish hedge."

the husband walked behind the plow. Wheeled transport was often difficult, as one retired grower remembers: "When anything needed moving from one area to another, we had sheets of old galvanise which we loaded with bags of bulbs and manure, and we dragged these along with ropes."

Soil slippage down steep slopes was a particular problem; during storms there could be landslides with soil and crops tumbling down the valley sides, burying more crops below. The earth-car came in useful here, with containers of soil from lower slopes being hauled back up to higher.

Flowering started in early February and continued through to May, with growers picking from up to fifty varieties. For most of the valley's history, flowers were picked when fully open, with white flowers going in blue-paper-lined boxes, yellow in green. During the

Old varieties have been collected and planted out in meadow and orchard areas around Cotehele House in the Tamar Valley, where visitors to the historic property can also admire and learn about the daffodils and the social history of the local flower industry.

1960s though, London flower wholesalers began to put pressure on the growers to change to picking flowers in bud, which meant that they took up only half the volume and did not need quite such a high level of protection in transit. Despite the opposition of many growers, the practice quickly took off, to become universal.

During World War II, national regulations were introduced to turn ornamental plant production facilities over to food. As a result many of the daffodils were dug up and thrown into the hedges, but, being daffodils, many survived and spread, resulting in the rich array of heritage varieties that can be seen growing along roadsides and hedge bottoms today. Regulations forbade the transportation of any ornamental crop, even in private baggage! Under the Transport of Flowers Act 1942, two London hauliers were jailed for six and twelve months, respectively, for carrying 138 boxes of flowers, including daffodils, leading to a public outcry. Some Scilly Isles growers, however, decided to fight back, sending some daffodils to Prime Minister Winston Churchill, who apparently declared, "These people must be allowed to grow their flowers and send them to London, they cheer us up so much in these dark days." In March 1943 the transport ban was lifted. Problems remained though—not enough boxes, chief among them. One grower has vivid memories of this time: "We were reduced to using waxed cardboard boxes that had contained meat for the American soldiers. . . . The stench when these boxes were opened was horrendous and it was not unusual to discover a slice of rotting beef adhered to the box . . . but the daffodils still sold well during the war years, despite the poor presentation."

The 1960s saw a rapid decline in the market garden industry in the Tamar. Increasing rail freight charges and the pulling up of smaller railway lines across the country made the distribution of the flowers much harder. Glasshouses and polytunnels elsewhere in the country and in the Netherlands began to compete. By the end of the decade the growing business was almost over. Grass, scrub, and tree seedlings began to take over the steep slopes of the gardens, and the packing sheds and houses where workers might take a break or brew a kettle fell into disrepair. The daffodils carried on blooming, as daffodils do, until the shade of brambles and trees reduced their flowering and eventually suppressed them altogether. Those in hedgerows (where many had been dumped during the war) fared better, as there is always some light, at least coming in from the side, resulting from regular cutting and pruning.

Today however, we have a good record of the Tamar Valley fruit and flower business. One reason is that a number of projects have sought to record the memories of retired local growers, with several books published telling their stories and including vintage photographs. Fortunately too, there has been an obvious local centre—Cotehele, an estate belonging to the Edgecumbe family and now run by the National Trust, a heritage conservation body.

The orchard at Cotehele.

Back in the 1960s, a group of local growers donated some daffodils to Cotehele, where they were planted out in areas of grass in the garden, itself a well-established and much-loved visitor attraction. Part of the Trust's mission at Cotehele was the preservation of the knowledge of local social history and so, eventually, attention turned to the daffodils.

In the early 2000s, led by the head gardener at Cotehele, John Lanyon, heritage daffodils were dug out of hedgerows and ditches and planted out in the orchard of apple and cherry varieties, which had also been important crops here. In 2003, an old packing shed was re-erected in the garden and furnished as it would have been during the daffodil-growing heyday. The shed was made of corrugated iron, a material which previously would have been condemned

for its ugly utility; many garden visitors enjoyed the irony of watching the National Trust, a byword for genteel good taste, put up such an "eyesore." Inside, audio recordings of retired growers were made available for visitors to listen to.

Identifying old varieties was a major headache but largely solved through the involvement of Kate Donald and of Dan du Plessis until his death in 2001. Now visitors can come and admire the delicate beauty of pale cream 'Sunrise', primitive doubles like 'Butter and Eggs', and the grandeur of 'Emperor'. Quality Daffodils, the business run by Ron Scamp, has also got involved and is making it possible for the Trust to sell bulbs of heritage varieties to visitors.

Breeders and Conservers

DAFFODIL PEOPLE

In 1910 the Rev. W. Wilks was astounded to find nearly 2,500 names in the RHS List of Daffodil Names. "Amateurs are already satiated with the multiplicity of extravagantly priced varieties," he wrote, wonderingly. "Is there anything in the same line which so greatly exceeds the old, old, Gloria Mundi? Is there anything . . . so greatly in advance of Emperor, Empress, Horsfieldii, [or] Barrii Conspicuus?"

It is a burning question. Why do people continue to breed plants after an acceptable garden plant has been produced? That there is always room for improvement might be one answer: plants can be bred for a longer flowering season, earlier flowering, stronger stems, better scent, disease resistance. Such factors explain the commercial focus of some breeding programmes. There is also the desire to perfect, like that of the craftsman who feels that nothing they make is ever quite good enough. Additionally there is the desire to create novelty, based on bringing together characteristics from different daffodil varieties or species, typically a characteristic from a minority-interest or culturally difficult species or variety and a more robust and easy-to-grow one. Undeniably there is an element of personal obsession, and it is this obsession which makes the daffodil truly a cult plant, one lifted beyond the natural or the functional or merely beautiful, but the object of a constant unfulfilled longing for the unattainable.

Here we will look at the process of breeding and the work of some modern breeders, but beforehand it might be interesting to look at some of the aesthetic issues involved. What flowers people like is a personal matter, and the gardening public and daffodil devotees are clearly divided. Personal preferences and indeed passions are aroused primarily over two issues: flower size and flower shape—in particular, how far flower shape deviates from the daffodil "norm."

Nearly all the breeders I spoke to agree that the public are wanting smaller daffodils, partly because many now garden tiny urban plots or can only plant in containers. There is also a strong tendency towards an appreciation of the natural-looking across the gardening world; smaller daffodil varieties may be no more "natural" than large ones, but they tend to look it. In some ways this can be seen as part of a wider movement, which values the traditional, the local, and the supposedly authentic, against the modern, the hi-tech, and the corporate.

Among modern daffodils there are several trends which spark particularly vehement reactions of antipathy: large flowers, doubles, and Split-coronas. Some flower sizes are now so big (in excess of 10cm/4 inches) that to many of us they look not only artificial but ungainly, as if familiar flowers had been fed on steroids. Doubles always stir strong emotions, with a minority of gardeners disliking almost any doubles. Double daffodils seem to evoke particular venom, possibly because the classic image of the flower is one so strongly associated with nature and the romance and simple beauties of spring. Thanks to its cup, the daffodil has a unique shape among flowers, and for many of us, once it loses this distinction, it loses its raison d'être and its soul. Although we know that nearly all the daffodils we see along roadsides are planted, there is part of us which wants to believe that they are wild—which we cannot believe if they are double.

It is Split-corona varieties, however, which earn particular hatred; for many of us, the splaying out of the cup is the grossest denial of the whole essence of what a daffodil is about. Split-coronas are very much a modern development, with very few being known before the 1950s. 'Buttonhole' was one of the first, bred in the Netherlands in the early 1920s; Mrs. Backhouse produced one around the same time, which she called 'Joker'—which perhaps illustrates what she thought about it. "They look as if they have been flattened with a rolling pin"; "Daffodils which resemble a pancake ought not to be exhibited" are two of many comments which veteran breeder Brian Duncan has collected over the years; he himself eventually decided he liked them enough to register around twenty varieties during the 2000s. Matthew Zandbergen probably spoke for many in the daffodil community when once he said, "Let there be no racial prejudice in our daffodil family."

Ron Scamp

CORNWALL

FOR RON SCAMP, "Cornwall is the world centre of the daffodil business. It's a perfect climate for them—we can have them in flower from December to the end of April, and sometimes longer." Ron's company, Quality Daffodils, currently offers far and away the largest selection of varieties anywhere, ranging from new hybrids to heritage cultivars snatched from the jaws of extinction. Ron was brought up on a family flower farm in the Tamar Valley; his uncle was Dan du Plessis, who became his mentor when he started growing, breeding, and showing in the 1970s. "It was as a hobby at first," he recalls, "but it became an obsession and, in the 1990s, a business." At first his company offered seven hundred varieties but now has around three thousand.

Ron says that he breeds new varieties "for the discerning gardener, with the cut-flower grower a good spin-off." Good plants, he says, "have to have good foliage, a strong stem, and a good bud which opens well." Although his stated goals in breeding are new colours, new combinations, and improved colour intensity ("Most of all I would like to breed a white with a red trumpet"), he values "the strength of flower and stem [as] the first criterion"—in other words, "it does not matter if a cross has a wonderful flower: if it can't stand up straight, it's no good . . . Scent is nice, and it helps in going back to the species for scent . . .

Resistance to fusarium is also important; vulnerability to this disease is a problem with deep genetic roots. Research into isolating the gene responsible is possible, but there aren't funds currently available."

Like all hybridisers, Ron also breeds "for show": "Exhibitors are the shop window for tomorrow's commercial varieties." Once a variety has proved itself as an exhibition plant, other possibilities open up, primarily the cut-flower trade and mass propagation for public and private gardeners. There is a relationship between these two aspects of the trade—it is not as if they compete for the same bulbs: "The flower growers need predictable top-quality bulbs, but their rejects are still quality and often end up in garden centres."

Patience is a primary virtue among daffodil breeders, even more than is usual in plant breeding. It takes at least four years to get a daffodil to flower from seed and, Ron says, five years' evaluation after that "before even thinking about naming it—and, if you have been propagating it, there could still be only fifty to sixty bulbs by [then]."

Well before a variety starts to appear in florist's shops or garden centres, it has to be, in the key phrase of the whole plant-growing business, "bulked up." Bulking up is the process of starting with one plant and ending up with however many are needed for a commercial launch, which in the case of daffodils means hundreds of thousands. With some plants this can be done very quickly, but with daffodils, the process is still slow. One day, no doubt, laboratory-based biotechnology will enable us to go from novelty cross to garden centre pin-up in a few years, but not yet. Traditional propagation techniques, and the real skill involved in applying them, is what lies between the breeder's cherished new plant and the brown paper bag or plastic net of bulbs which the amateur gardener pulls open in hope and expectation as they prepare to plant them. "The Dutch are the master propagators," explains Ron, "especially for garden varieties. Chipping is the main means of propagating—one bulb can be cut into six to eight pieces, each producing three or four bulbils, which can flower in three years' time. Once they are big enough they can then be chipped, and the process goes on . . . If all goes well, it is possible to go from one to 100,000 in ten years using chipping." This is considerably faster than relying on natural increase.

So, in the end, it takes at least a total of thirteen to fifteen years for a new variety to get into specialist commercial

A selection of Ron Scamp's daffodils. 'Trecara' (2001) **1**, a Small-cupped variety for mid to late season, which illustrates well what the daffodil breeding of the twentieth century focussed on—solid perianth segments of "good substance," well able to withstand handling and forming a full and relatively flat background for the corona. 'Rebekah' (1997) **2** is a late-season double. 'Saint Day' (2000) **3** is a mid-season dwarf Triandrus. 'Katherine Jenkins' (2007) **4** is a mid-season Jonquil.

production. It may take still another decade, and possibly longer, before it becomes plentiful and cheap enough to make much of an impact on the amateur market. This process is a very indeterminate one, as unlike many other plants, where quick-to-propagate plant varieties can be fast-tracked from breeder's bench to market in a few years if a company decides to promote it, the slow pace of daffodil production is much more market-led. And many variables will affect a new variety's reception at each stage:

- Has it inspired enough exhibitors to continue to show it from among all the other new varieties?

- Has it continued to win prizes?

- Has it survived enough spring storms, outbreaks of disease, and other unpredictable events, with flowers still held high, to convince growers that it is more than just a pretty face at a show?

- Have enough dedicated growers bought and exhibited the plant to convince a grower to propagate enough bulbs to enable them to offer it to the mail-order bulb specialist? This is a crucial stage, as this is when a variety breaks out of the world of only being grown by daffodil enthusiasts, to being grown by keen gardeners, people like this writer, who grow a wide range of plants and like to integrate daffodils in amongst other plants that they grow. At this stage, a variety can often reach a kind of equilibrium, as a popular variety with keen

gardeners or perhaps cut-flower growers, but not really getting much further.

- Does its sales and its wider profile (write-ups in garden magazines, mentions in books, appearances on TV spring garden programmes, etc.) convince a major grower that the plant is worth bulk-propagating, in order to sell on to the wholesale bulb trade?

It goes without saying that the position of a variety on this ladder, from breeder's bench to garden centre bin, is very much reflected in price. New varieties, with real show potential, can sell for as much as £50 each. This may sound a lot to most gardeners but is much less than the early years of the twentieth century, as was seen with 'Fortune'. Even varieties listed in catalogues by the 1920s could be selling for as much as £900 at today's prices. Interestingly, a high price for a new variety seems to have been a very poor predictor of future value; there is no relationship between a bulb's being expensive in the listings of the leading supplier of the time (Barr & Sons) and its future popularity, its likelihood of winning an award from the RHS, or even its survival.

Ron has registered around three hundred new varieties, across all divisions. He has produced some fine doubles, such as 'Heamoor' (1996), which has particularly neat and elegantly arranged petals, the rich yellow 'Gossmoor' (2000), and the orange-centred 'Madam Speaker' (1998). This last was named for the first woman Speaker of Britain's

House of Commons, Betty Boothroyd; it is, Ron notes, "as robust as the lady, stands up well to the elements, and [is] admired by all who see it." He has also bred some Jonquils, like 'An-Gof' (1999), with a green, yellow, and orange cup ("the first of this colour in the division"), and some Split-coronas ("which appeal to the cut-flower trade"), such as 'Jack Wood' (1997), a variety he calls "probably the best show form flower in this division we have yet—rich golden shades with a flat corona of slightly darker tone with a touch of orange at the rim." Both this and 'An-Gof' are vigorous and increase well—both absolutely essential for a commercial future. In his ongoing breeding, Ron says how he is "going back to the older Poeticus hybrids." Reaching back into the past is a common pattern in many areas of plant breeding; it tends to happen when breeders feel they have reached a plateau or need some more material to work with.

Like most breeders I spoke to, Ron sees a definite trend towards dwarfer daffodils. "There are," he notes, "a lot of interesting miniatures, but also too many which are not garden-worthy, often derived from Iberian species." Having had failures with several Alec Gray miniatures myself, I understand. In sum, Ron echoes what at least three other people mentioned to me in the course of researching this book: "Everyone is after the next 'Tête-à-Tête'," he says—and adds, tantalizingly, "I've got a feeling that Harold Koopowitz is sitting on it."

Ron is keen to stress how he sees "the daffodil world as a unique fraternity, a bit of keeping secrets but people are very free with pollen and pretty open about their methods—breeders are very competitive, but in a friendly way." To the outsider, one new variety may look much like another; Ron himself is almost inclined to agree: "I've named daffodils and sometimes seen someone else's and you can't tell the difference." As with other plant species with high public profiles (particularly roses), there are demands from various quarters to name new varieties for publicity purposes. In 2008, for example, Ron named a plant 'Marie Curie' for the cancer charity's Diamond Jubilee, and in 2008 'Undeb Rygbi Cymru/Welsh Rugby Union' for the sporting organisation, who perhaps predictably planted it out at their national stadium in Cardiff.

There is one intriguing little coda to Ron's breeding programme. It is possible to buy his new varieties for very little money, in fact at bargain basement prices. There is a catch, however: there is no way of identifying them! During the lifting and grading process, some bulbs get rejected—they are healthy but too small for him to bother growing on, or they are varieties he has decided not to carry on with, or they fall out of trays or in other ways lose their identities. These discarded bulbs are sent off to a commercial grower, who then grows them on for three years, before selling them. "We call it the rainbow mix," Ron says. "People do not know what they are going to get—could be some very good new ones, but there is no easy way of knowing them." In 2010 he reckons he sold some 450 bags this way, each of one hundred bulbs.

Elise and Richard Havens

HUBBARD, OREGON

NOT SURPRISINGLY, Elise Havens, daughter of key American breeder Grant Mitsch, has been hybridising daffodils since her college days. She started out as a computer programmer "in the early days of computing," while her husband, Richard, was a science teacher. "In 1978," she says, "we decided to go full-time. We were mid-thirties, we bought a farm—my father had put out his fiftieth catalogue, and we bought the business off him." She describes the climate of her home region—the Pacific Northwest—as "ideal." Much of the hybridising done in the United States happens here, in fact, but "the region has been relatively late to start shows, although they are surprisingly widely distributed across the U.S."

Elise agrees with many other breeders in her feeling that "the trend is very definitely for smaller plants." She continues, "My father did a lot of miniatures and upper divisions—the U.S. has historically had a longer interest in upper divisions than most other countries—and new miniature varieties sell out very fast." Although the Havenses work with a very wide range of daffodil varieties, their interest clearly remains with these smaller-flowered plants. Sterility is often a problem with the upper divisions: if a hybrid is sterile, its genetic material cannot be taken any further, and so it becomes a dead end. As Elise describes it, "We are trying to use fertile varieties to widen the colour range; in Jonquils particularly, we have got some good pinks and yellows in recent years. [E]arlier I did more work in division 3 [Small-cupped], trying to get some more pinks, and to develop a true red—also, reverse bicolours." So far, Elise and Richard have registered nearly three hundred varieties.

Aesthetics can take a breeder only so far. In fact, it should perhaps be said that a breeder who works exclusively with the visual qualities of their plants will never achieve much. Physical resilience is important, and disease resistance particularly vital. Elise and Richard found that 'Daydream' (a reverse bicolour Large-cupped, registered by Grant Mitsch in 1960), which had been the cornerstone of their breeding programme, increasingly began to suffer from basal rot. "And so we had to move on plant health and find varieties resistant to fungi." With Jonquils, Elise is working on improving the form of the plant and, as with all the upper divisions, to widen the colour range.

Some of the varieties which Elise and Richard Havens feel best express their work. 'Emerald Empire' (Large-cupped, 1998) **1**, "one of our favourites of the green eyes—the very white flower with symmetrical form is a real beauty in our opinion." 'Oregon Pioneer' (Large-cupped, 1995) **2** explores the possibilities of a pink and yellow in combination. 'Perpetuation' (Jonquil, 1995) **3**, "one of our fertile Jonquils which has done exceptionally well in shows and in the garden; it is a considerable improvement over 'Pipit' [a popular Jonquil], one of my father's flowers from the early 1960s."

"It's a challenge," says Elise. "There are so many things to be done . . . I have an innate love of the flower, I've had it all my life. I want to improve it. It's important for us that we have plants that are excellent garden plants and not just good show flowers." She counts intuition and experience as the most important things in the breeding process but allows that scientific information is increasingly vital. Knowledge of chromosome counts is especially important for upper divisions, as if chromosome numbers do not match up between two potential "parents," then successful pollination is impossible.

Among Brent and Becky Heath's output of new varieties are 'Katie Heath' (2002) **1**, a Triandrus, selected for being long-lasting and sturdy; 'Baby Boomer' (2008) **2**, a short-growing Jonquil with five to ten flowers per stem and very fragrant; and 'Golden Echo' (2003) **3**, another Jonquil, of average height and a strong grower. 'Tiny Bubbles' (2009) **4** is a complex cross, so counts as a Miscellaneous variety; very dwarf at only 15cm (6 inches), free-flowering, and fragrant, it is the kind of variety which the Heaths see as having a great future in small urban gardens.

Brent and Becky Heath

GLOUCESTER, VIRGINIA

BRENT AND BECKY HEATH have one of the most comprehensive ranges of bulbs for sale in the United States. Daffodils, though, are the core of the business and their real passion. Brent in fact is the third generation of his family in the daffodil business. He describes how his grandfather, Charles, who was living in Massachusetts at the time, ate a cantaloupe for breakfast and loved it so much, he tracked down the grower in Virginia. He went to visit the grower, to schedule regular deliveries of the fruit, and while he was there, noticed large colonies of daffodils in the area; they had established from early introductions and grown so extensively that local people were cutting and sending them off to the cities. He too got into the bulb and cut-flower business, but, having worked in the U.S. consular service in Europe, he was familiar with more modern varieties, with longer and stronger stems, so he began to import bulbs. Brent's father, George, had one of the largest collection of daffodils in the United States by the time Brent was born. His passion for daffodils was passed on to Brent, and the boy quickly became an expert.

Later in life, Brent became friends with Grant Mitsch, who took the young man under his wing, showed him the business, and passed on his knowledge of hybridisation.

The Heath family business is basically retailing, buying in bulbs from growers around the world and with whom they have built relationships; indeed, they have trial gardens in both the Netherlands and Virginia, where blooming time, reproduction rate, and other key aspects of plant performance can be noted. They undertake some breeding but are very clearly focussed. "A younger generation of gardeners is downsizing with daffodils," says Becky. "They want smaller, neater plants, to grow in containers that fit into their smaller homes and to have them among perennials." So far, Brent and Becky have registered around thirty varieties, many of these being Jonquils, which have always been important in the American South. "We concentrate," says Becky, "on developing very strong plants, with more fragrance, and we are more interested in great garden plants than just good show plants."

Robert Spotts

OAKLEY, CALIFORNIA

"**I HAD NEVER SEEN** a daffodil until 1975, when I was nearly forty, as I was born and lived in the Arizona desert," reports Bob Spotts. "When I moved to northern California, I was really taken by daffodil forms and started growing them. I met Sidney DuBose [another prominent U.S. breeder], who became my mentor and encouraged me to start hybridising [and] through Sidney I met Manuel Lima, a recluse, whose solitary aim was to create a green daffodil—I was very taken with Manuel's seedlings and have worked on this for over fifteen years."

The green daffodil is only part of Bob's breeding programme; he has named around thirty-five varieties, across a wide range of divisions, with one in particular, 'Kokopelli' (1993), a miniature Jonquil with rounded tepals, being a particular commercial success.

Bob believes he has more with potential in the pipeline.

Bob is a retired mathematician who had worked as an education programme analyst. "Hybridising," he says, "I consider to be an art rather than a science. As a mathematician I appreciate symmetry; it's very important to me. For example, I like to work on spider daffodils." These are varieties with narrow perianth segments, which go against a strong, long-term trend in breeding towards full, rounded flowers. "Sometimes," he says, "there is a mismatch between what show judges like and what the public likes."

The quest for a green daffodil may seem an eccentric one, but in fact there is a green species, *Narcissus viridiflorus*, very often tagged "mysterious." From the

Of Bob Spotts's highly innovative breeding, 'Kokopelli' (1993) **1** is the best known representative, a mid to late season dwarf Jonquil. 'Spider Woman' (2006) **2** is an early to mid season Small-cupped, named, as is 'Kokopelli', for a Navajo deity. This unnamed seedling **3** is a good example of Spotts's adventurous work, the result of a cross between the relatively conventional Small-cupped 'Triple Crown' with a hybrid of 'Actaea', an old Poeticus variety, and *Narcissus viridiflorus*. Plants with such a wide genetic base could represent the future for daffodils.

mountains of southern Spain and North Africa, this is an autumn-flowering plant with star-like and intensely fragrant flowers of an odd murky green. In cultivation it has proved somewhat erratic, although Bob points out that its blooms last for a long time and it appears to do well in central and southern California. With viridiflorus genes, Bob can work at both the green colour and the spider shape. Among the varieties he has produced using *N. viridiflorus* have been 'Spider Woman' (Small-cupped, 2006), yellow with an orange corona, and a very distinct star shape; and 'Mesa Verde' (Large-cupped, 2001), with a distinct greenish tinge. 'Spider Woman' is named for the goddess in Navajo creation mythology. Many of Bob's names reflect an interest in the Southwest and its rich Native American heritage.

"The drive," says Bob, "is to create something extremely pleasing, but also recognition." There have clearly been hard times, as he warns other breeders: "I learned by bitter experience to keep your plants on your own land, otherwise terrible things can happen . . . I had plants on someone else's property once and lost about ten years' work through their being carelessly destroyed." Now, at this stage in his career as a breeder, he seems to be creating a genuinely distinct look, one which even those new to the daffodil world might be able to recognize as having a very personal stamp on them. He recalls the words of a renowned orchid and daffodil breeder: "Harold Koopowitz once said to me, 'Don't get in line, create your own line.'"

Harold Koopowitz

NORTH TUSTIN, CALIFORNIA

HAROLD KOOPOWITZ is interesting and unusual as a breeder in that he is a plant scientist by profession—Professor Emeritus of Ecology at the University of California at Irvine, after having spent a lifetime working on plant reproductive biology, applying this to both ornamental horticulture and conservation.

He describes himself as having always been interested in plant life ("I was fascinated by bulbs as a child; I remember asking my mother how you make new plants"), and he found daffodils "particularly alluring." As a graduate student, he "imported some bulbs from Holland[,] one of which was 'Newcastle' [a 1957 Large-cupped bicolour]; I was blown away by the flower, and thought I must get more of these." A classic book on daffodils—Michael Jefferson-Brown's *Daffodils and Narcissi* (1969) was a major inspiration, and it was reading this that convinced him he should have a go at breeding. "It's fun and creative," he says, "but you are gambling—it's like playing roulette, but it takes five to six years for the wheel to stop spinning."

Harold got side-tracked into orchid breeding (*Paphiopedilum*, slipper orchids), a commercial venture, and "neglected daffodils for twenty years." When he got back to them he made a wise decision; realising that he could not compete with Grant Mitsch and Brian Duncan (a leading Northern Irish breeder), he decided to "go back and do things differently." He identified two areas where new daffodil breeding was needed. One was the handful of autumn-flowering species, whose potential had almost never been tapped, possibly because they come from a region with a climate different to others (mountain areas with dry summers); another was

A selection of Harold Koopowitz's breeding. An unnamed seedling **1**, this clone is typical of daffodils that have 'Emerald Sea' in their background. 'Emerald Sea' was originally made by John Hunter in New Zealand, and Harold has used it extensively to make autumn-flowering hybrids. Another unnamed seedling **2** descended from 'Emerald Sea', whose green coloring and reflexed tepals come (originally) from *Narcissus viridiflorus*. 'Itsy Bitsy Splitsy' (2007) **3** is a rare example of a dwarf Split-corona; it has been recognized with the Brian and Betty Duncan innovation award from the American Daffodil Society and the Ralph B. White medal from the RHS. 'Puppy Love' (2007) **4** is a dwarf, of which Harold says, "Miniatures with this coloring, form, and small size in Large-cupped are almost unknown—the corona coloring develops to a salmon pink."

the scope for breeding miniatures, where he saw a capacity to express a far wider range of colour and form.

A knowledge of reproduction ecology and access to biotechnology facilities enables Harold to do things which other breeders cannot—for example, to take sterile varieties and convert them to fertile polyploids. At one stage he tried "embryo rescue," a technique which has proved very useful in crop plant breeding, but he confesses that "when the results flowered, they were disastrous."

Another reason that Harold Koopowitz is unusual among daffodil breeders is that he has experience with breeding other plants. "I took an orchid approach to breeding—if you get stuck, look around for some new species to breed in . . . Don't stay in one track."

Breeding for Harold is "science and art interacting: you use the science for creating new material but then aesthetics takes over. You breed towards a goal, but the nearer you get towards a goal, the more difficult it becomes to achieve it." Several varieties are being commercially trialled, out of nearly forty he has registered.

Preserving the past
HEIRLOOM DAFFODILS

THE APPRECIATION AND CULTIVATION of old varieties, "heirlooms," has become an important part of the current garden scene, on both sides of the Atlantic. The pioneer here was Graham Stuart Thomas (1909–2003), who worked for the UK's National Trust for many years; his work with old roses brought many back from the cusp of extinction and did a great deal to popularize them. Names become separated from plants with remarkable ease, as any gardener will know. Bulbs, however, present particular problems, as they disappear so totally for much of the year, so labels go astray even faster than with perennials or woody plants.

Ron Scamp started collecting old varieties many years ago: "Despite scepticism from colleagues, I thought they were important to keep, at least the pre-1940 varieties. I've now got several hundred." These are not just an important breeding resource but also a part of the business, as his catalogue now has a section for heirloom varieties.

The most systematic collectors of old daffodils are Kate and Duncan Donald, who live and grow their plants in the incredible natural beauty of Loch Ewe on the northwest coast of Scotland. Rows of daffodil clumps are lined up around their croft house and an impressive wind turbine—a reminder that although the climate here is very mild, the wind is a big part of life.

Kate had a childhood love of daffodils, which was rekindled by a scholarship year at Tresco Abbey Gardens on the Scilly Isles in the late 1970s. In 1983 she became RHS Daffodil Registrar, and because of this was asked by the National Trust for Scotland to create a National Collection of daffodils at Brodie Castle. "I was always more interested in the older varieties," Kate says. "They still come up in gardens decades after they have been planted, which shows they are survivors and therefore proven, unlike modern show varieties, which are an unknown quantity. They have an unsophisticated charm . . . and softer, more luminous colours."

Duncan adds, "We got interested in making a collection of old daffodils in the 1980s. [At the time] I was curator of the Chelsea Physic Garden in London [and] we had some bad storms then—a large tree blew over on top of a heritage daffodil collection—it really focussed our minds."

The Donalds made 1935 the cut off point for their collection. Why? Kate explains: "This was when 'Fortune'-derived varieties began to become important—'Fortune' was such a breakthrough in colour that it was used extensively to breed new cultivars, and so there was an explosion in new orange-cupped cultivars, which are very similar in colour and form, and therefore hard to distinguish and identify." That leaves around seven thousand named varieties, of which the Donalds now have four hundred plus. "We began to spend a lot of time looking at derelict cottage gardens, and then to ask garden and estate owners for bulbs (mostly when visiting on Scotland's Garden Scheme open days), and started to build up a reference collection—people were so often very generous," says Kate. While visiting the Donalds, I stopped off at a graveyard with them in the old fishing village of Ullapool, but was relieved they left their spade in the car.

In 1990 the couple moved to Scotland, and as Duncan puts it, "The children got used to the Easter holidays being daffodil time and endless garden visits." Scottish gardens have often preserved the past better than English ones, and with the climate being a good one for daffodils, they have proved a fruitful territory for tracking down long-forgotten varieties. As time has moved on, and the daffodils have grown, the Donalds are able to offer a number for sale—wide distribution is always a guarantee of survival. "We want to do for narcissus what Graham Stuart Thomas did for roses."

One particular property, Threave in Dumfries and Galloway, has been a "Rosetta Stone" for them, says Duncan. The property had been owned by the Gordons, a family of Liverpool industrialists, who had used the castle as a summer residence. They had regularly bought bulbs over a long period and,

crucially, kept good records. In the 1960s, a set of notes were made of the old head gardener's knowledge, which included a sketch map of the woodland area indicating where old daffodil varieties were planted. The Donalds were then in an excellent position to identify daffodils growing in the garden; so far, they have named about ninety. A new breakthrough is in rescuing old varieties which were grown in Scilly as cut flowers, before the industry settled down to concentrate almost exclusively on Tazettas. This is going to be "now or never," as so-called conservation measures are subsidising farmers to plough up old fields with their daffodils to plant them with wildflowers, and even to clear daffodils out of hedgerows. Kate is also trying to record something of the knowledge and expertise of Keith Low, a fisherman and semi-retired flower farmer, whose family has farmed in Scilly for generations. In 2012 she saved fifty-seven varieties from Scilly, although Keith reckons that some he remembers have been lost for good.

Over the years, the Donalds have worked out an effective methodology for identifying varieties in old gardens. They have systematically gone through old nursery catalogues, held by the RHS's Lindley Library in London, and assembled a database mapping the availability of varieties over time. "The collections for sale in the catalogues are particularly

Daffodil grower Ron Scamp in his field of heirloom daffodils near Falmouth in Cornwall. ▶

valuable," explains Duncan, "as these would have been bought in bulk and therefore most likely to still be around in gardens. [I]f a garden is known to have been planted up at a particular date or between two dates, then it is possible to go to the catalogue database, and see what was available, narrowing down the possibilities. [M]agazine articles (e.g., *The Gardeners' Chronicle*) can be a useful source of information about when a particular garden was planted up if the garden itself has no record." Gardens which do keep archives may sometimes contain invoices from nurseries or bulb dealers, listing varieties, or there may be old catalogues with names marked up. "Illustrations are the key," says Kate. "It is impossible to name an old daffodil with any certainty if we cannot compare a specimen with two or three images from an old catalogue or plates in a gardening magazine."

There is no doubting the rigour of the Donalds' approach. The changes in names resulting from the way daffodil classification systems have worked over the years and duplications in naming have resulted in much confusion. "We are very careful," says Duncan. "Every clump is mapped, and has an aluminium label with the name and accession number impressed onto it, and another label is buried with the bulbs, which themselves go in an onion bag, so the roots

can grow out but not the bulbs." He goes on to explain that flowers are systematically photographed, at different angles, and at different times—as flowers can change in appearance considerably over the period in which they are in flower. The eventual aim, apart from making as many varieties available for sale as possible, is a field guide to old daffodils, which will enable anyone to identify old garden varieties.

'Bath's Flame' (Engleheart, pre-1913) , an heirloom with the propellor-type petals typical of many late nineteenth-century varieties, now made commercially available again by both Ron Scamp and the Donalds. Kate and Duncan Donald's croft  on the northwest coast of Scotland, home to a major collection of heirloom daffodils and a small nursery. Identifying daffodils requires much careful close examination, comparison of flower colours with the RHS colour chart, and reference to illustrations in old books . ▶

2

Gone Native

DAFFODIL COLONIES
AND HOTSPOTS

Splashes of yellow in spring on roadsides or in hedges mark where someone once planted daffodils, or on the other hand perhaps abandoned them as garden refuse. Places with daffodils away from roads may indicate where once upon a time someone lived and gardened, the flowers coming up every year like a ghost, long after the timber of the house has rotted or the stones and bricks have been grown over. Throughout Britain and Ireland, and to a lesser extent, the United States and New Zealand, daffodils regularly survive over many decades.

The flowers really do have a remarkable ability to cope with the competition of other plants, being defeated only by anything which grows taller and shades them—even then, they may carry on growing for many years without flowering.

Of the temperate world's floral spectacles, it is bulbs which provide some of the best: English bluebells and snowdrops; cyclamen and crocus in many places in southern Europe and Turkey; and of course wild daffodils. Truly wild daffodils can be spectacular in France, but perhaps the finest display is in the valley of Khust, in Zakarpats'ka Oblast in Ukraine, where a Poeticus type flowers on the very edge of the range of the species, in vast quantities. Beyond their natural range, a number of bulbous plants have naturalised: species which are introduced to a location with a climate not too dissimilar to that in their native land, and which have a strongly perennial character, and which, crucially, reproduce to form clumps. Snowdrops have taken to woods in the British Isles and in the Netherlands, creeping out from cultivated populations. So have daffodils, as they have also done in some places in the United States. Britain's two species of "wild" daffodils are almost certainly introductions of great antiquity. There is a population of *Narcissus obvallaris* around Tenby in south Wales, and a widely scattered number of *N. pseudonarcissus*. Theories abound regarding the origin and distribution of these. We have seen that there is

possibly a link with Medieval monasteries; a Roman introduction has also been suggested.

Daffodils which have "gone feral" tend to form localised colonies— hotspots. Unlike most garden plants, which simply get swamped and die out in the face of more robust and better-adapted native vegetation, daffodils keep on coming back; their ability to grow early in the year gives them an advantage, particularly vis-à-vis grasses. Hybrids, or "unnatural" variants like doubles, seem to survive just as strongly as species, although they do not usually seed. The ability of such "unnatural" garden varieties to survive and slowly spread among native vegetation is almost unique among garden plants; double snowdrops (*Galanthus nivalis*) are one of the few others. Their constantly coming back reminds us annually of long-forgotten gardens and growers.

The sixteenth-century barber/surgeon, herbalist, and writer John Gerard wrote that daffodils grew "almost everywhere through England," which is often quoted to suggest that the plants have been hugely reduced in numbers over the centuries. No one else mentions their having been common, however,

At Acorn Bank in Cumbria, "wild" *Narcissus pseudonarcissus* **has naturalised alongside daffodil cultivars which were planted in the 1930s. They have cross-bred to produce a range of flower shapes and sizes. It is debatable whether modern daffodil varieties would have the same capacity to similarly hybridise.** ▶

and the evidence of their naming suggests that they were never particularly well known. The colourful pockets of the plant at high density strongly suggest that they are an introduced species; however, like much of the European flora, they were almost certainly native in Britain before the Ice Age.

Among the populations of garden daffodils which have "gone native," 'Telamonius Plenus' is particularly interesting. An old double variety (pre-1620), it has been reported from nearly sixty different places in old gardens across Britain, in some cases appearing to disappear and then reappear, possibly because repeated mowing early in the year so weakens the bulbs that they stop

flowering, and then with leaves which are so similar to grass, they become practically invisible. An example was its flowering for the first time in living memory in 1995 on the National Trust–owned Gibside estate near Newcastle-upon-Tyne in northern England. An early introduction to the United States, it is also known from several old east coast American gardens.

Of all daffodil hotspots, the most mysterious are the populations of daffodils associated with the Cherokee Nation in the United States, specifically in Oklahoma. Areas associated with the Cherokee are rich in *Narcissus pseudonarcissus* and several old varieties, including 'Telamonius Plenus' and 'Butter and

Eggs' (pre-1777). One well-known site is a cemetery near a late nineteenth-century Cherokee courthouse at Saline in the northeastern part of the state. Another is the Ross Cemetery, near Park Hill, where John Ross is buried; Ross was chief of the Cherokee Nation at the time of the infamous "Trail of Tears," when ethnic cleansing by the U.S. government drove the Cherokee from their homeland in Georgia and neighbouring states. It is thought possible by some daffodil experts that the Cherokee brought the bulbs with them, as they were well established in the eastern United States by the time of the expulsion.

The most predictable hotspots are of course in places which have always been gardens. Here, however, they can still raise questions. The spectacular drifts at Acorn Bank, a property owned by the National Trust in Cumbria, northern England, encompass both *Narcissus pseudonarcissus* and a variety of hybrids. Does the *N. pseudonarcissus* date back to Medieval times, when the area was an

outpost of the mysterious Knights Templar order? The mix of hybrids is known to date back to the writer Dorothy Una Ratcliffe (1887–1967), who bought the property in 1934. One theory is that she bought a job-lot of "rejects" from the Backhouse family, in which case many unnamed crosses or stray unidentified bulbs would have ended up being planted here. Heirloom daffodil experts Kate and Duncan Donald, however, think that this is unlikely. They have a term for this kind of mix—"Spanish meadow," arguing that many wild forms were imported into Britain in the late nineteenth and early twentieth century, by dealers such as Barr, and that these have cross-bred with *N. pseudonarcissus* over

'Telamonius Plenus' (also known as 'Wilmer's Double Golden Daffodil' and 'Double Van Sion', among several others) is an old English variety, dating back to the early seventeenth century at least. It is capable of surviving and spreading over time through bulb increase (i.e., perennialising, not naturalising, which involves seeding), and there are some colonies which may be centuries old.

the years, and some older varieties, to produce what plant ecologists call a hybrid swarm, a complex mass of continually hybridising individuals, much as is sometimes found naturally in Spain with wild species.

Gardens around the homes of well-known breeders from daffodil history are also fascinating places to wander and see a variety of flowers. Nothing is identified, and so it is impossible to tell whether you are looking at a plant that went on to a great future or was used for further breeding or simply thrown out as inadequate but then took root and thrived. The Rev. Engleheart's old garden at Little Clarendon in Wiltshire in southern England is one such well-known place for daffodil lovers. The small size of the flowers, compared to modern ones, ensures that they fit into the country scene. Daffodil enthusiasts can wander around and look for the varieties for which Engleheart was famous, often not finding them, but instead finding flowers that are almost but not quite the right ones. It is a living illustration of the breeding process, a collection of plants from which winners were chosen, but where the losers did not die on the compost heap as they do with the rejects from most breeding programmes.

The Golden Triangle
THE BIGGEST AND OLDEST DAFFODIL HOTSPOT

THE WILD DAFFODILS of the English Lake District, with their Wordsworth associations, are the most well known. The largest concentration, however, is the area around the town of Newent and the villages of Dymock and Kempley on the Gloucestershire/Herefordshire border, dubbed the "Golden Triangle" early in the twentieth century. Quite why the plant should be here in such huge quantities is impossible to say; at some stage the plant must have appeared and then had better opportunities to survive and spread than elsewhere. One reason must surely be to do with the fact that for much of the post-Medieval period there has been a relatively high proportion of open woodland, its preferred habitat. Where woodland is kept open through selective felling and coppicing—both traditional management practices—conditions are perfect for certain bulbs: wild daffodils, wild garlic (*Allium ursinum*), and English bluebells (*Hyacinthoides non-scripta*). The reason is that there is enough shade to suppress grass but enough light early in the year for the

bulbs. Grazing, by sheep, cattle, or pigs, also helped reduce the bramble, the greatest enemy of bulbs.

The Gloucestershire/Herefordshire border area had long had an association with fruit growing, largely for the production of cider (hard cider to Americans) and perry (an equally alcoholic version made with pears). During the nineteenth century, fruit growing greatly expanded, as now the arrival of railways allowed growers to send their fruit off to the rest of the country, where an increasingly wealthy population was beginning to eat a healthier diet.

By the late nineteenth century a wildflower became an economic resource, as daffodil flowers could now be sent to local markets. Daffodil production became a by-product of fruit-growing—the grass below the trees would be cut in late summer to make it easier to pick windfalls, which ensured that there would be reduced grass competition when the flowers emerged in spring; they would also be easier to pick. After World War I, Toc H, a Christian service organisation, promoted the picking of daffodils to cheer up hospital patients, and also began to sell daffodils at hospitals to raise money. Commercial picking also took off, especially since flowers were usually available for Mothering Sunday (the fourth Sunday of Lent), traditionally the beginning of the gardening season in Britain.

During the late nineteenth century and early twentieth, the income from

FARNDALE
NATURE
RESERVE
WARNING
IT IS FORBIDDEN TO
PLUCK OR INJURE
THE DAFFODILS
PENALTY £5

Narcissus pseudonarcissus genuinely naturalises, in that it seeds vigorously, with plants flowering in five years from germination; old churchyards are a favourite place, especially given the recent wildflower-friendly management trend—as here, wild daffodils at Jesus Church, Troutbeck, Windermere, Cumbria **1**. *Narcissus pseudonarcissus* in Farndale in the North York Moors National Park in northern England attracts tens of thousands of visitors every year **2**.

picking daffodils actually became quite important, as it was the only independent income for agricultural labourers in the area, doubly welcome for it being at a time of year when there were few other sources of income. Others joined in too, especially Gypsies and casual workers from the Midlands. The flowers became an early tourist attraction, with a special Daffodil Line train running between the villages and the nearby town of Newent. Visitors came from the Midlands, and from the conurbations of South Wales and Bristol. However, with the closure of Dymock Station in 1959 and the line being pulled up, interest flagged for several decades.

The 1960s and 1970s were a bad time for the daffodils, as they were for wildlife and wildflowers generally in Britain. Rising populations and rising meat consumption globally drove agricultural intensification. Many orchards were ripped up and converted to arable (largely for grain and potato production), so the daffodils were increasingly being limited to the hedges. This was also a period when local governments started to "tidy up" road verges, cutting the vegetation in May or June, just as the daffodils were about to set seed. The invention of nylon cord brushcutters was

more bad news—now country churchwardens could ensure that the unruly grass around gravestones in churchyards was kept tidy, too.

From the 1990s onwards appreciation of the daffodils began to grow again. With more and more walkers crisscrossing the fields around Dymock and Kempley, "daffodil teas," which had been held for over fifty years by local village churches to raise money, became increasingly popular. The tourism potential of the area at daffodil time has now been fully recognised, with pamphlets showing the best places to see the flowers and a circular walk of 14km (9 miles) along local footpaths around some of the best locations. Now over three thousand people descend on the area over two weekends in late March and early April. Flowering time depends on the weather, so occasionally the events have to be rescheduled.

It is thought the Farndale daffodils originated with the monks of nearby Rievaulx Abbey. Though this photo would suggest their numbers are secure, they are protected, and the public are banned from picking them.

A number of initiatives have focussed on conserving the daffodils, notably the Golden Triangle Wild Daffodil Rehabilitation Project, coordinated by a local garden designer and environmental campaigner Chris Bligh. Since 2003 volunteers have systematically recorded wild daffodil locations, collected seed, and worked with local landowners, such as the Forestry Commission, to improve habitat in woodland owned by them. Since 2010, with funding from the National Grid (an energy infrastructure body), the Golden Triangle Project is working to re-create a mile of daffodil and wildflower habitat along roads and footpaths around the villages at the centre of the area. Seventy-five local people have undertaken to each grow a thousand daffodils in plug trays, so that young plants can then be planted out in selected road verges and community locations such as churchyards, eventually to flower and seed themselves further.

Raising awareness of the flowers and their correct management is also an aim. Churchyards in particular have seen some spectacular recoveries of daffodils and other wildflowers, as the awareness of them as wildlife sanctuaries has grown, and management regimens changed to become more flower-friendly. The bulbs can survive for many years as part of pasture or occasionally mown grass, even if prevented from flowering; so that once a field or churchyard is managed properly, former daffodil fields can recover, and more visitors to the Golden Triangle can appreciate the sight of thousands of pale yellow flowers spattering the spring grass.

Narcissus pseudonarcissus grows in large numbers in a variety of habitats in the area around Newent, Gloucestershire, with open woodland, roadsides, and orchards being particularly favoured places. Highway embankments are now being colonised, too; indeed it is an irony that these places, so inhospitable to us, are now among the best wildflower habitats in Britain. ▶

Daffodils
in the
Garden

A great many daffodils are planted thus: 1) dig hole, 2) throw in bulbs, 3) replace soil. They go on to thrive, as did many of those flung into hedges during wartime, when flower producers had to go over to food production. Daffodils are survivors, and their popularity is undoubtedly linked to their being so easy, vigorous, and indestructible.

A little care, however, reaps greater rewards, while a little understanding of the plant's natural cycle helps us appreciate why certain practices are helpful and others not.

Soil, situation, early growth, and planting

THE IDEAL SOIL for daffodils is a deep well-cultivated fertile loam with plentiful humus, and moisture from autumn until early summer at least. The abundance and health of daffodils in damp west coast climates like Ireland and Cornwall does indicate how much constant moisture is appreciated. Poor drainage is not, however, and can result in a variety of fungal diseases causing decay and death. Those who garden on badly drained land, where water stands for long periods on the soil surface, should consider growing daffodils in raised beds.

Although daffodils appreciate fertility, the level of plant nutrients in most soils is enough for their requirements. On very poor or thin soils, additional phosphorus and potash may be needed, supplied by slow-release fertilisers such as bonemeal. Generous helpings of stable or farmyard manure, as beloved by traditional gardeners, are not necessarily beneficial and might even cause problems, with excessive nitrogen leading to soft, sappy leaf growth. Compost from well-decayed plant waste is a better way of adding humus to soils without high levels of nitrogen.

Daffodils need light but can be grown in the partial shade of deciduous trees, open woodland being the natural habitat of some species. Too deep a shade, and they may start to come up "blind," i.e., all leaf and no flower. Flowers will turn to face the sun, which is something to be borne in mind when planting.

Unlike bulbs from more continental climates, such as tulips and the tall "drumstick" alliums, daffodils start root growth early, in late summer or autumn. They do, however, need cool conditions to initiate this growth, below 12.7c (55F), and at least six weeks between this temperature and freezing. During this time there is a change in the chemistry of the bulb, which produces chemicals that act as an anti-freezing agent, enabling them to survive soil freezing. In an ideal world, bulbs would be planted in August, but bulb companies rarely make them available until September. The sooner they can be planted the better, with November being the latest advisable for areas with mild or cool winters, such as northern Europe or the American West Coast; however, in regions with severe winters, where soils freeze to great depth, such as much of the American Midwest or Northeast, planting must be done by mid-October, otherwise the "antifreeze" process will fail, and bulbs may be destroyed by ice crystals forming in them.

When planting, a good rule of thumb is that the depth of soil above the neck of the bulb should be twice the height of the bulb. In situations where frequent soil cultivation is likely, they can be planted deeper. Breaking up the soil at the bottom of the planting hole helps them to root down quickly. Bulbs will eventually find their own depth and those who have got involved with heirloom daffodil projects and start to dig up old clumps will observe how deep the bulbs can be. How far apart? If an instant group effect is wanted, they can be planted 5 to 7cm (2 to 3 inches) apart, but it will be only a few years before their growth will cause crowding. Ten to 15cm (4 to 6 inches) is generally regarded as a sensible compromise between a group effect and giving them plenty of space. If a variety is known to be slow to increase, it can be planted more tightly. As will be discussed, very sparse planting may be appropriate in borders dominated by perennials.

Labelling bulbs is important if there is any desire to know the names of plants when they flower or are lifted and divided in future years. Labels easily get lost, broken, or rendered illegible, and because there is no branch to tie them to, or clump of roots to stick them into, labels get detached from bulbs with great ease. Aluminium or copper labels are the only ones which are truly indestructible and can be written on with simple pencil—on thin metal, the action of writing impresses the text, so making it very long-lived indeed. If the label is attached to a long, thin piece of wire, it is possible to mark clumps of bulbs very securely; this method also allows the label to be held securely close to the soil surface, if the wire is plunged in deeply enough. Those who are especially concerned to avoid identity crises can mark planting positions with plastic rings buried just below the soil surface to surround small clumps—these can easily be made by hacksawing up old plastic flower pots. The cognoscenti plant their bulbs in plastic nets to make absolutely sure that varieties do not get muddled.

An alternative to labelling is mapping, which removes the danger of physical loss of labels. Mapping systems tend to be very personal, but even the most basic, that of making a note of what varieties were planted in what border, helps. Nowadays, with pictures of most varieties available online with a few keystrokes, identification of a small number of varieties when in flower is easy, if they can be checked against even something as simple as a list.

Spring and early summer

AN EARLY GARDENING LESSON for many people goes something like this: "Don't cut daffodil leaves off, or they will not flower next year." It's true that the foliage, which stays green after flowering, is feeding the bulbs, to build them up with nutrient stores for next year. Embryo flower buds are formed during the summer, too. Cutting leaves or tying them reduces the time and the ability of the plant to feed the bulbs, and however annoying it is to have clumps of increasingly tatty leaves in the border, stay there they must until they become at least half yellow—which sometimes may not happen until a month or so after Midsummer's Day. Clearly there are planning and design issues here, and there is much which can be done to help hide the leaves (see "Daffodils in borders"). On the other hand—and contrary to popular opinion—picking the flowers does no harm, at least if the stalk is cut, rather than pulled.

Growing daffodils in grass

DURING THE LATER YEARS of the nineteenth century, it became popular to grow daffodils in grass, a situation for which their lifecycle suits them (unlike tulips, for which this treatment guarantees a one-year wonder). Drifts of bulbs emerging in spring from among grass creates the illusion that the plants are growing wild, evoking Wordsworth's Lake District experience. The idea (originally Barr's) was given a boost by William Robinson, whose book *The Wild Garden* (1870) gave permission to a whole generation to turn their backs on the excessive order and formality of the Victorian era's gardening. The practice became known as "naturalising"—a term that is perhaps misleading, as it implies that a plant propagates itself by seed to become a semi-natural self-sustaining member of a plant community. In fact, daffodils almost never self-sow in rough grass, or do so only very intermittently; rather, they simply build up progressively bigger clumps. "Perennialise" might be a better term.

Many people's enjoyment of daffodils is through mass plantings of bulbs in grass in public parks or along city or suburban roadsides. This can be achieved

Daffodils flourish best in grass if it is mown during the winter to reduce competition **1**. 'Princeps' and other old varieties in grass at Great Dixter, Sussex **2**; plantings here could be some of the oldest deliberately naturalised daffodils in Britain, as the owners, at the turn of the nineteenth and twentieth centuries, were friendly with Gertrude Jekyll, who was among the first to advocate the practice. A wide variety of daffodils can be naturalised; these are in the orchard at Cotehele in Cornwall **3**. ▶

in the garden too, and not only with the full-size varieties usually used, but also with smaller varieties and species. A number of points need to be made, however, if long-term success is to be achieved.

The daffodils will start to grow at the same temperatures as the grass, just keeping ahead of it, so it helps if the grass is cut short before the daffodils emerge, by the winter solstice at the latest. It should also be obvious that the grass should not be cut until the daffodil foliage begins to yellow, which may mean several weeks of increasingly long grass, and that cutting long grass will leave a bald yellow look after a such a late cut—beauty does require compromises!

Choose which daffodil varieties to grow in grass wisely—the best to use are ones known to be vigorous, which rapidly build up clumps. Most bulb catalogues are helpful in indicating suitable varieties, usually describing them (again, not with the best term) as "naturalising well."

Deceptively frail-looking, *Narcissus bulbocodium* can be naturalised successfully in grass over a moist soil, as here at RHS Wisley, Surrey. A low-fertility soil will reduce grass growth and be beneficial to the bulbs.

Daffodils in borders

THE COMBINING OF BULBS with perennials in borders is a perfect way to ensure interest in spring, when the majority of perennials are only just waking up. The two are complementary in that while one is in active growth, the other is almost dormant—at least above ground. Deciduous shrubs too offer the possibility of a similar complementary relationship, but only if the shrubs are pruned in such as way as to create enough space beneath them for bulbs to grow unimpeded by branches and be seen.

The main problem with co-habiting perennials and bulbs is that of leaf remains after flowering. Clumps of daffodil leaves can be large and, as they slowly yellow, singularly unattractive in the border; and if groups are large, the mass of soggy, collapsing foliage may even crush smaller perennials. There are a couple of possible ways to reduce this problem. One is to grow daffodils behind vigorous, early developing perennials, such as species of *Geranium*, whose clumps of fresh growth and flowers will hide the daffodil foliage. Another is to not grow daffodils in clumps, but to scatter them as individuals—most will soon begin to form small clumps in any case.

'Jack Snipe' growing beneath a cherry tree at Broadleigh Gardens, Somerset, a nursery which specialises in small-growing bulbs. The area around tree bases is often unsuitable for grass growth, but spring-flowering bulbs are able to take advantage of good spring light.

'February Gold' with *Leucojum aestivum* and *Scilla sibirica* in a woodland garden. Daffodils are frequently grown alongside other spring-flowering bulbs to create attractive early colour combinations, the space being later occupied by summer-flowering perennials.

Long-term prospects

DAFFODILS INCREASE over time, so that one bulb produces smaller offsets around its base, which in time grow and have more offsets. Eventually large clumps build up, even to the extent of plants becoming clearly crowded with reduced flowering. At this stage, digging them up—or, as it has traditionally been known, "lifting"—is advisable, preferably after they have become dormant but before new root growth has started, generally during the mid-summer months. Bulbs can then be separated and replanted in new positions.

The speed with which daffodils build up to form clumps varies enormously. In the past, this speed controlled the rate at which the bulbs could be propagated and thus made commercially available. In recent decades, twin-scaling and chipping—two methods of cutting bulbs into small pieces and growing them on in nursery beds—have speeded up propagation. In the garden, most amateur growers will be happy enough with natural rates of increase, but they soon appreciate that speed of increase is extremely variable, with some varieties taking years to produce divisions while others rapidly form impressive clumps.

Daffodils grow well in light shade among woodland plants such as *Anemone nemorosa* in situations where shade reduces growth by later developing species. Seen here are *Narcissus pseudonarcissus* **1** and 'Charity May' **2**.

Growing indoors

AS SIGNS OF SPRING, daffodils are appreciated as indoor plants, flowering much earlier than they would do outside. As such they should be regarded as temporary, to be planted outside as permanent garden plants once they have finished flowering. Bulbs need to be planted in containers at high density, so as to maximise the impact of the display, with just their noses visible above the surface of the compost. Any freely draining material sold as potting compost is suitable, although if the variety is a more valued one, it is worthwhile using a quality material, to ensure good nutrition for flower production for next year.

Bulbs must be kept cool and in good light until they are clearly about to flower, as premature heat can result in buds aborting—the bulbs need chilling to stimulate flowering and healthy growth. Once inside, maximum light is important, as even in the best conditions indoors, the lengthening of the stem caused by the plant stretching for light during a relatively dark time of year is always a problem. Tying the stems to light supports is often necessary.

Some daffodils are sold for Christmas flowering. The types of Tazetta sold as paperwhites will flower without compost, simply with the bulbs sitting on pebbles in a dish of water, within weeks of starting growth. Some other scented Tazettas, such as 'Grand Soleil d'Or',

are sometimes sold specially treated to ensure that they will flower quickly. Despite their tall stems, other Tazettas make good indoor plants, particularly since their flowers are so heavily scented. In principle any daffodil can be persuaded to flower indoors, although in practice smaller varieties are often more practicable and attractive.

Small daffodils tend to do well in containers as there is less stem and fewer long leaves to flop about. They can be brought into heated rooms (although the lighter and cooler these are, the better) to flower at the end of winter and planted out later to give many years of pleasure in the garden. Seen here are 'Jetfire' AGM (Cyclamineus, Grant Mitsch, 1966) **1** and 'Tête-à-Tête' **2**.

Idiosyncrasies

THE OVERWHELMING MAJORITY of daffodils are hybrids, and as with all plants, hybrids are easier to grow than species; the simple process of selection in garden conditions selects for clones of easy cultivation, while a major concern of almost all hybridisers is to produce robust, easy-to-grow plants with no particular likes or dislikes. With daffodils there are a few exceptions. On the "no fuss" side, Poeticus types and *Narcissus pseudonarcissus* seem particularly tolerant of year-round wet soil, but they also appreciate summer moisture, as do Small-cupped varieties (which have a high proportion of Poeticus genes) and Jonquils. Cyclamineus types have a tendency to prefer cool acidic soil, moist but well drained; the smaller the plant, the more acid the soil needs to be—reflecting the preference of the original species for woodland conditions. In regions with hot summers, Triandrus and Cyclamineus prefer some summer shade.

Tazettas are the most demanding, as the original species from which this group is derived hail from regions that experience hotter and drier summers than other daffodils, so their needs are closer to tulips—the plants will not repeat flower unless they have a hot dry summer to "bake" the bulbs; they are also less hardy. Jonquils too appreciate hot summers, but they are less demanding of them than Tazettas.

Most daffodil varieties are hardy down to USDA hardiness zone 3 or 4. Tazettas should be regarded as zone 5 minimum, although the Poetaz types, which actually includes most of the varieties widely available, are generally hardy to zone 4. True Tazettas in northern Europe may be hardy but need a warm and sheltered location to do really well, so they are ideal for borders on south-facing walls.

High summer temperatures or early and warm springs have an impact on daffodils. Trumpets tend to perform better in USDA zones 3 to 7, and so are less successful in the American South and similar climate zones in central to southern China and southern Japan. In these regions, Jonquils and Tazettas are particularly successful, with *Narcissus tazetta* actually naturalising (in the true sense of the word) in Japan, even growing by the coast down to the high tide mark. Jonquils have a particular association with the American South, where they are known as "sweeties." Areas which rarely experience frost (zone 9 and above) can be regarded as difficult, although there have been some successes in growing daffodils in Florida.

These unidentified Tazettas are growing in a sunny spot on a bank in the Tamar Valley. If given a warm and sunny spot, many Tazettas will flourish and bulk up well over the years; they are much less tolerant of cold positions or climates with cold winters.

A trial of daffodils at RHS Wisley. The outcomes of trials are invaluable to gardeners and landscape managers looking for trouble-free varieties. The very best plants may be awarded the Award of Garden Merit (AGM).

Pests and diseases

MOST GARDENERS who grow daffodils have few problems with pests and diseases. Slug damage to buds, causing flowers to open shredded, is about the worst which most experience.

With whole acres devoted to a single crop, commercial growers are much more vulnerable to pests and diseases. In 1917 a disease began to seriously affect many British growers. Leaves became stunted and distorted, and hundreds of acres were lost; some growers were ruined. It turned out to be a microscopic nematode, or eelworm. The Royal Horticultural Society coordinated a research effort led by James Kirkham Ramsbottom, then only twenty-five years of age, at RHS Wisley, near London. He discovered that the eelworms were killed by a simple-sounding but actually quite demanding treatment—a four-hour soak in water at 43.3C (110F). Less than four hours or just under this temperature, and some eelworms survived; slightly hotter, and the bulbs would be damaged or killed. The addition of a small amount of formaldehyde, then commonly used as a sterilising agent in horticulture, helped ensure a one hundred percent kill. The treatment also works against another major pest, narcissus bulb fly. Cornish breeder and grower P. D. Williams was one of the first to apply the hot-water treatment; one of the varieties whose starting stock was saved was 'Carlton'. Ramsbottom, however, tragically died a few years later, at the age of thirty-three.

Growers went to considerable and ingenious lengths to build facilities to treat large quantities of bulbs with hot water. One Tamar Valley smallholder, Fred Rogers, got hold of an old boiler from a tin mine to inject steam into large tanks of water, which he ran for about six weeks every summer. Being successful, he started to treat bulbs for other growers and went on to buy a purpose-built oil-fired boiler with electric hoists for lifting bulbs in and out.

Narcissus bulb fly maggots hollow out the centre of the bulb, causing blindness (all leaf, no flower) and sometimes bulb death. Commercial growers can use insecticides, but there is nothing available to amateur growers, at least in Europe. Ron Scamp sees narcissus bulb fly infestation as his main problem: "It can be treated chemically, but I don't— you just have to accept it." The solution adopted by most growers is that fundamental standby of good farming: crop rotation. "We rotate," says Ron. "Only two years for one crop of daffodils and then five to six years without." Commercial daffodil growers often rent their fields from more conventional farmers, who grow wheat, barley, potatoes, or pasture grass. Amateur gardeners can help avoid the problem by growing daffodils in cool, shady places—the fly seems to prefer plants in warm situations.

Basal rot, caused by a fusarium fungus, is another major problem for some growers and gardeners, especially on damp soils. It has probably all but wiped out many historic varieties, as there is considerable variation in resistance. Breeding fusarium resistance into new cultivars is something which is very much on the agenda for some breeders, but progress on this front is slow.

Viruses too are a problem for growers and, again, some varieties are much more severely affected than others. Commercially important varieties can be "cleaned up" through micropropagation in the laboratory; this has been done, for example, with 'Grand Soleil d'Or' in the Scillies. For domestic gardeners, however, viruses are rarely a problem.

PLANT LISTS
SELECT BIBLIOGRAPHY
SOURCES AND RESOURCES
PHOTO CREDITS
INDEX

Plant Lists

THE BEST ALL-ROUND, TRIED AND TESTED

Whether the varieties in this first of four best-of-the-best short lists are "classic daffodils" or "big, bold, and brassy" is a matter of opinion.

Carlton AGM (Large-cupped)
Dutch Master AGM (Trumpet)
Golden Rapture AGM (Trumpet)
King Alfred (Trumpet)
Kingscourt AGM (Trumpet)
Marieke (Trumpet)
Saint Keverne AGM (Large-cupped)

White varieties in the Trumpet, Large-, or Small-cupped divisions:

Ben Hee AGM (Large-cupped)
Broomhill AGM (Large-cupped)
Empress of Ireland AGM (Trumpet)
Ice Follies AGM (Large-cupped)
Misty Glen AGM (Small-cupped)
Mount Hood AGM (Trumpet)

Other colour combinations in the Trumpet, Large-, or Small-cupped divisions:

Badbury Rings AGM (Small-cupped)
Fragrant Rose (Large-cupped)
Glenfarclas AGM (Trumpet)
Irish Minstrel AGM (Large-cupped)
Lemon Glow (Trumpet)
Passionale AGM (Large-cupped)

The best of other divisions:

Actaea AGM (Poeticus)
Cantabile AGM (Poeticus)
Chinita (Tazetta)
Dove Wings AGM (Cyclamineus)
Falconet AGM (Tazetta)
Hoopoe AGM (Tazetta)
Ice Wings AGM (Triandrus)
Jenny AGM (Cyclamineus)
Rippling Waters AGM (Triandrus)
Rugulosus AGM (Jonquil)
Tuesday's Child AGM (Triandrus)

REVERSE BICOLOURS

The following varieties offer an intriguing colour mix and are most reliable.

Binkie (Large-cupped)
Dickissel AGM (Jonquil)
Intrigue AGM (Jonquil)
Pineapple Prince AGM (Large-cupped)
Pipit AGM (Jonquil)
Spellbinder AGM (Trumpet)

HEIRLOOM VARIETIES, PRE-1930

All are readily available and easy to grow.
Barrii Conspicuus (Small-cupped)
Bath's Flame (Small-cupped)
Coverack Glory (Large-cupped)
Emperor (Trumpet)
Fortune (Large-cupped)
Horace (Poeticus)
Lucifer (Small-cupped)
Princeps (Trumpet)
Sir Watkin (Large-cupped)
Sulphur Phoenix (Double)
Sweetness (Jonquil)

DWARF VARIETIES (MAX. HEIGHT OF 30CM/1 FOOT)

Bantam AGM (Large-cupped)
Cornish Chuckles AGM (Miscellaneous)
Founding AGM (Cyclamineus)
Hawera AGM (Triandrus)
Jack Snipe AGM (Cyclamineus)
Jet Fire AGM (Cyclamineus)
Kokopelli AGM (Jonquil)
Little Gem AGM (Large-cupped)
Pencrebar (Double)
Rosemoor Gold AGM (Jonquil)

Segovia AGM (Small-cupped)
Silver Chimes (Tazetta)
Snipe (Cyclamineus)
Surfside AGM (Cyclamineus)
Tête-à-Tête AGM (Miscellaneous)
Narcissus bulbocodium AGM
Narcissus cyclamineus AGM
Narcissus triandrus 'Albus'

GOOD FOR NATURALISING

The following varieties are particularly good for naturalising—or more accurately, perennialising, as they increase rapidly. Note that the species have the capacity to truly naturalise, through seeding.
Apricot (Large-cupped)
Carlton AGM (Large-cupped)
Feeling Lucky AGM (Large-cupped)
Ice Follies AGM (Large-cupped)
Princeps (Trumpet)
Telamonius Plenus (Double)
Thalia (Triandrus)
Tresamble (Triandrus)
Trevithian AGM (Jonquil)
Narcissus obvallaris AGM
Narcissus poeticus var. *recurvus* AGM
Narcissus pseudonarcissus AGM

GOOD FOR GROWING IN POTS INDOORS
Charity May AGM (Cyclamineus)
Cheerfulness AGM (Double Tazetta)
Erlicheer (Double Tazetta)
Geranium AGM (Tazetta)
Tête-à-Tête AGM (Miscellaneous)
Yellow Cheerfulness (Tazetta)
Narcissus papyraceus

EARLY BUT ROBUST, EVEN IN CONTINENTAL CLIMATES
Aberfoyle AGM (Large-cupped)
Avalanche AGM (Tazetta)
Boslowick AGM (Split-corona)
Bram Warnaar AGM (Trumpet)
Bryanston AGM (Large-cupped)
February Gold AGM (Cyclamineus)
Grasmere AGM (Trumpet)
Itzim AGM (Cyclamineus)
Little Beauty AGM (Trumpet)
Monal (Large-cupped)
Peeping Tom AGM (Cyclamineus)
Rijnveldt's Early Sensation AGM
  (Large-cupped)
Sagitta AGM (Trumpet)
Whipcord AGM (Jonquil)

FOR WARM SPRINGS AND HOT, HUMID SUMMERS

Where sun-resistant flowers are vital (e.g., the American South), the following varieties are good.
Accent AGM (Large-cupped)
Barrett Browning (Small-cupped)
Ceylon AGM (Large-cupped)
Gigantic Star (Large-cupped)
Merlin AGM (Small-cupped)
Minnow AGM (Tazetta)
Mount Hood AGM (Trumpet)
Notre Dame AGM (Large-cupped)
Pinza AGM (Large-cupped)
Pipit AGM (Jonquil)
Quasar AGM (Large-cupped)
Thalia (Triandrus)
Topolino AGM (Trumpet)
Narcissus jonquilla AGM

Select Bibliography

Allen, Natalie. 2000. *Full Circle: Memories of Cotehele Valley Market Gardeners and the Diaries of Joseph Snell*. Privately published.

Barnes, Don. 1987. *Daffodils for Home, Garden and Show*. Timber Press, Portland.

Besler, B. 2000. *The Garden at Eichstätt: The Book of Plants*. Taschen, London.

Bowles, E. A. 1934. *A Handbook of Narcissus*. Martin Hopkinson, London.

Brockbank, William. 1894. Edward Leeds. *The Gardeners' Chronicle* (10 and 24 November):561–562; 625–626.

Burbidge, F. W. 1875. *The Narcissus: Its History and Culture*. L. Reeve & Co., London.

Coats, Alice M. 1971. *Flowers and Their Histories*. McGraw-Hill, New York.

Davis, P. 1990. The Backhouses of Weardale, Co. Durham. *Garden History* 18(1):57–67.

Donald, K. 1984. Peter Barr, 1826–1909. *The Garden* 109:401–405.

Gerard, J., and M. Woodward. 1994. *Gerard's Herbal: The History of Plants*. Senate, London.

Herbert, W. 1846. On hybridisation amongst vegetables. *Journal of the Horticultural Society of London* 2:1–28.

Herbert, W. M., and Hamilton P. Traub. 1970. *Amaryllidaceae, with an Introduction by H. P. Traub*. Verlag Von J. Cramer, Codicote (UK) and New York.

Jacob, Joseph. 1910. *Daffodils*. T. C. & E. C. Jack, London.

Jefferson-Brown, Michael. 1969. *Daffodils and Narcissi: A Complete Guide to the Narcissus Family*. Faber and Faber, London.

——. 1991. The work of the Backhouse family. *Daffodil and Tulip Yearbook, 1990–1991*:48–51

Paravisini-Gebert, Lisa. 2009. [Jamaica] Kincaid speaks of daffodils . . . . *Repeating Islands*. repeatingislands. com/2009/06/01/kincaid-speaks-of-daffodils. Accessed 19 July 2012.

National Trust for Scotland. 1999. *Ian Brodie: A Chieftain in the World of Daffodils*. NTS, Edinburgh.

Rivera Nuñez, Diego, et al. 2003. The origin of cultivation and wild ancestors of daffodils (*Narcissus* subgenus *Ajax*) (Amaryllidaceae) from an analysis of early illustrations. *Scientia Horticulturae* 98(4):307–330.

Tompsett, A. 2006. *Golden Harvest: The Story of Daffodil Growing in Cornwall and the Isles of Scilly*. Alison Hodge, Penzance.

Uings, Joy. 2003. *Edward Leeds: A Nineteenth-Century Plantsman*. Ph.D. diss. University of Manchester.

Wells, James S. 1989. *Modern Miniature Daffodils*. Batsford, London.

Wheeler, D. 2007. The Brodie of Brodie: his life story and the search for his daffodils. *Daffodils with Snowdrops and Tulips*, RHS:42–46.

Wilson, A. M. 1939. Recollections of the early years of this century. *The Daffodil Yearbook*, RHS:19–22.

Sources and Resources

The Daffodil Yearbook, published under various names by the RHS from 1913 onwards, is an invaluable source of information on the plants, daffodil people, and daffodil history; on the subject of money specifically, it is interesting to note an article in its 1933 edition, "New and Rare Daffodils as an Investment." Since 2011, the yearbook is issued as *Daffodil, Snowdrop and Tulip Yearbook*.

The RHS-run International Daffodil Register and Classified List has a searchable online database: apps.rhs.org.uk/horticulturaldatabase/daffodilregister/daffsearch.asp.

Daffseek.org, run by the American Daffodil Society, is an incredibly useful data source for basic descriptions, pedigree, descendants, and often pictures; however, opinions differ on how accurate it is.

NATIONAL SOCIETIES

In some cases, notably in the United States, there are some strong regional societies as well.

American Daffodil Society
daffodilusa.org

The Daffodil Society (UK)
thedaffodilsociety.com

National Daffodil Society of New Zealand
daffodil.org.nz

Tasmanian Daffodil Council
tasblooms.com/tdc

Victorian Daffodil Society (formerly the Australian Daffodil Society)
daffodilbulbs.com.au/vds

SUPPLIERS OF DAFFODILS

It would be easy to fill up many pages with lists of daffodil suppliers. Now that it is so easy to search online for local or specialist nurseries and bulb dealers, links are given only for those who are featured in the book:

Kate and Duncan Donald
Croft 16
croft16daffodils.co.uk

Elise and Richard Havens
Mitsch Novelty Daffodils
mitschdaffodils.com

Brent and Becky Heath
Brent and Becky's Bulbs
brentandbeckysbulbs.com

Ron Scamp
Quality Daffodils
qualitydaffodils.com

DAFFODIL GARDENS AND COLLECTIONS

In the United States, the American Daffodil Society has approved display gardens, with an up-to-date list: daffodilusa.org/displaygardenprogram/approveddisplaygardens.html.

Daffodil collections, where plants are clearly labelled, have had a distinctly chequered career in Britain, with several appearing and then disappearing again over the last few decades. There are now very few places where it is possible to see labelled plants. The following have labelled collections based on particular breeders or historical periods.

GUY L. WILSON DAFFODIL GARDEN, Coleraine, Northern Ireland (National Collection)

KATE AND DUNCAN DONALD, Croft 16, Poolewe, Wester Ross, Scotland (pre-1930s varieties)

COUGHTON COURT, Warwickshire (Throckmorton Collection)

BRODIE CASTLE, Nairn, Morayshire (National Trust for Scotland)

BROADLEIGH GARDENS, Somerset (many miniatures and Alec Gray hybrids)

Many other gardens have good drifts of yellow (albeit usually unlabelled) and often a wide range of interesting or older varieties, among them:

ACORN BANK, Cumbria (National Trust)
CASTLE FRASER, Aberdeenshire (National Trust for Scotland)
ERDDIG HALL, Wrexham, Clwyd (National Trust)
FLORENCE COURT, County Fermanagh, Northern Ireland (National Trust)
GIBSIDE ESTATE, Tyne and Wear (National Trust)
GREENBACK GARDEN, Glasgow (National Trust for Scotland)
HOWICK HALL, Northumberland
KINGSTON LACY ESTATE, Dorset (National Trust)
RHS GARDEN WISLEY, Surrey
RYDAL MOUNT, Cumbria (National Trust)
SPEKE HALL, Liverpool (National Trust)
THREAVE GARDEN, Castle Douglas (National Trust for Scotland)
THE WEIR, Herefordshire (National Trust)
WESTBURY COURT, Gloucestershire (National Trust)

Finally, there are the expansive (and definitely unlabelled) views of daffodils "gone native." For information about visiting Wordsworth's daffodils in the English Lake District: nationaltrust.org.uk/aira-force-and-ullswater. To see daffodils in Farndale: farndale.org/daffy.htm. And to see daffodils in Gloucestershire's Golden Triangle: daffs.org.uk.

Photo Credits

Page 143, courtesy R. A. Scamp, Quality Daffodils.

Page 147, courtesy Elise J. Havens, Mitsch Novelty Daffodils.

Page 148, courtesy Jay Hutchins, Brent and Becky's Bulbs.

Page 150, courtesy Colorblends Flowerbulbs.

Page 151 (left), courtesy Kirby Fong.

Page 151 (right), courtesy Bob Spotts.

Page 152, courtesy Tom Stettner, Jr.

Page 153 (left), courtesy Harold Koopowitz.

Page 153 (right), courtesy Tom Stettner, Jr.

All other photographs are by Jo Whitworth.

Index